Containment Scenario:

DisloInter MedTextId entCation:

Horse Medicine

M. Mara-Ann

O Book • 2009

Profound gratitude to those who have inspired and supported the creation of this work including: Juliana Spahr, Leslie Scalapino, Stephen Ratcliffe, Walter K. Lew, Edwin Torres, Judith Goldman, Fred Frith, Maggie Nicols, Katherine Mezur, Joan Retallack, Carla Harryman, Marc Bamuthi Joseph, Molly Holm, Maggi Payne, Pauline Oliveros, Carol Wolf, Terry Riley, Jennifer Nellis, Ananda Bagiackas, Katrina Rodabaugh, Erika Staiti, Lara Durback, J.D. Mitchell-Lumsden, Jennifer Dearinger, Jeremy James Thompson, c.marie.smith, Dillon Westbrook, Samantha Giles, Jacob Eichert, Heather Jovanelli, Rene J. Scheys, Elizabeth Brock, min kollega och vän Anna Sparrman for finessing my Swedish, and Travis Ortiz for his always generous intellect and creativity.

Grateful acknowledgement to the editors of *Cricket Online Review*, *Shampoo, and The Walrus* where parts of this work have appeared.

Copyright © 2009 Marcie Ann Fuller
ISBN: 1-882022-67-X   Price: $15
Interior book design and typesetting by M.Mara-Ann
Cover design by Leslie Scalapino and Amy Evans McClure

For

my grandmother, Carol Fuller,
who lulled me to sleep as a child with
bed time stories and nursery rhymes

and

my parents,
Judith Ann Johnson and Ellis Ray Fuller,
who shared their love and enthusiasm for
the wilderness with me.

CONTAINMENT SCENARIO:

DisloInter MedTextId entCation:

Horse Medicine

Introduction	11-16
Prologue	17-20
Act I	21-47
Director's Notes	48
Anterior Technical	49-58
Monologue	59-62
Act II	63-105
Director's Notes	106
Soliloquy	107-115
Act III	116-155
Director's Notes	156
Epiloque	157-160
Posterior Technical	161-173
End Notes	174-186
Works Cited	188

Introduction

in the Messaging of speech

to tell the telling of telling as this is the relative
a stating of liberation to impossible suffering
driving the hour of hours where a telling must imply
an ultimate tale of describing the will wanting this
and the stationing hours of hour for eventual modalities

> upon arriving at the summit, the field was filled
> språket befinner sig i framtiden i den tiden då
> *[the language stands in the future in the time of]*
> the dogs were every color, shape, and size
> den kallas för (il futuro) säger kvinnan
> *[it's called the future says the woman]*
> three german shepherds had already passed
> tvärtom she wonders was once there was being
> *[the other way she wonders was once there was being]*
> running the other direction – the largest was
> och den negativitet i frågan om att ge liv
> *[and the question of negativity about giving life]*
> two younger dogs were following close behind

considering considerations to consider in candor

the living adequately well among practical ways of lessening

a living's living doing the states holding encapsulated

when there wants a causing to direct knowing instead

relational relationships in relating rightly to be surmised

where a watering water's where waters is garden gaining

    the smallest dog was only twelve inches tall

    trädet stod framför hela sagan – på sidan
    [the tree stood before the whole story – on the page]

    wore a stiff wire muzzle twice as large as

    halvvägs upp och utsträckt mot väst
    [up half way and stretched out towards the west]

    wearing a protective device around his nose

    inte alltid, men ibland kan det vara
    [not always, but sometimes it can be]

    among the sea taller, he carried the weight

    stor och rund när sovandet sker på dagen
    [large and round when sleeping during the day]

    as if it were natural for the smallest to be

in the time of time timing time speaking truths discovery

sounds to simplify the more charged breathing to taste

an essential bringing discrimination creating community crux

control granting mind's tendency towards failure in sense

speaking and the good of speaking to one's good other not
object attention in mindfulness to gradually die knowing
the look at looking to see no side of seeing sight self leading
the moment of delirium becoming aware of abiding in essence
this being a being of good speaking to time being timed in

    in the left peripheral sight a hawk emerged
    men det var det inte – kanske på grund av vinden
    [but it wasn't – perhaps because of the wind]
    flying from the left emerging and circling right
    förmånga stod nere på marken – eller luften
    [too many stood down on the ground – or the wind]
    signing to tell of watching what closely
    ingenting i trädet förutom trädet sträckte ut sig
    [nothing in the tree except the tree stretched out]
    three dogs passed, two twins playing with
    mönstret berodde på stark vind, (fa freddo)
    [the pattern depended upon strong wind, very cold]
    growling and biting marked larger irritation

rivering a river following courses constant following for very
the sounds of deepening pleasure waking the informal quite
the great speaking of greatest swiftness flowing past passing
reminding regard outside of the calm of watch shouting
there those them willing to be speaking wills there for fear

the quality before experienced thought of precious wasting
a willing who gaspingly wills the trying grasping ways off
an informal catching opportunity to change close attention
to them who graspingly will willingly feel feeling torn at will

    passing the mark, the black dog following

    nästa dag – tidigare -- solen sken
    [the next day – earlier – the sun was up]

    the referee pulling by the ears, innocence

    hundarna var avslappande bara med två – en vita
    [the dogs were relaxed with only two – a white]

    the golden dog to bear irritation's insult

    den öppna gatan varmare än innan
    [the open street as warmer than before]

    signing a stark lacking of consent in one least

    (solamente una) det finns, men sovande
    [only one there is, but sleeping]

    yet, the evidence of flight cast further

the river's wandering destined destination of river destining
a purification visualized in front which describes interchange
to let letting to push speaking speech letting off into pushing
watching the return of three emotional places distracting
in keeping our kept keeping of destination seeing sight to open
involving the letting otherwise transform breath called object

holding spoken speech above the bottom water's holding push
an effective indication of concentration purifying image
to see sight seeing them who are destining our sight vision

    no hawk envisioning a sign of telling circling
    att leva som om det var överallt
    [to live as it was all around]
    the eating hour delayed by at least two
    utan det kan vara samma med, men valet
    [without, it can be the same together, but the choice]
    a later relevance with each pasing circle
    tala om – (intrappolare) på toppen
    [talk about – trapped on the top]
    boys of eleven as if before there was pivot
    den vita hunden betydde äldre utan år och färg
    [the white dog meant older without years and color]
    just like any other year so telling not this

nothing noting to converse taking not speech personal
persisting happening with painful meditation opposite guilt
the spoken spiraling concentration growing in the halting way
timing the time of times in timing devise telling over time
powerful experiencing minds in lethargy longing to resolve
a gathering gathered of speakers speaking self gathered out
the focusing thoughts nearing fantasy to dull feelings beginning
to converse banishing struggling from language vocabulary

light falling in rings helping in nurture

andas upp och ner vägen klättrade runt
[breathing up and down the road round climbing]

the repetition to solve elevations design

var försiktig eftersom allt händer runt trädet
[be careful as all happens around the tree]

a hill causing a river of degradation during

rygg och armarna med liten kunskap
[back and the arms with small knowledge]

bracing through multiplicity with pitch

kommer fram mot den flygande sagan
[coming forward toward the flying story]

a maturing vision to scale difficulty

we always do doing the must being being in constant doing
close natures to impress idiosyncratic anticipations turning
and celebrate speech spoken celebrations celebrating resolve
where occupants greet through intensities approaching waste
we us conversing that one of that waiting for being clearly clear

Prologue

A Running Horse Veiled

Two horses left standing down. Two down left standing in legacy. Two downed legacies left horsing in the shade. Two forms horsing in the shade of standing. Two shaded forms standing for legacy. Two legacies shading forms standing down. Two lost shades horsing to the left of legacy. Two horses standing in the shade of legacy. Two empty horses lost standing in fabrication. Two shades of horses forming standing.

Two forms of fabrication leaving down. Two downed legacies emptying form. Two shadows left fabricating horses. Two forms of legacy leaving down. Two fabricating shades of horsing left. Two empty horses of fabrication standing. Two veiled legacies fabricating down. Two horses leaving veils in shading form. Two shades downing the legacy of fabrication. Two down left veiling the horse of emptiness. Two legacies standing in veiled fabrication. Two shaded legacies fabricating horses. Two horses veiling in shadows of emptiness. Two forms emptying fabrications of veils. Two running horses

LEFT DOWN FABRICATING. TWO ILLUSIONS OF FABRICATION VEILED IN LEGACY. TWO HORSES LEGACIES IN THE SHADE OF ILLUSION. TWO VEILS LEAVING FABRICATION TO LEGACY. TWO DOWNED ILLUSIONS FABRICATING HORSES. TWO EMPTY FORMS DOWNING VEILED RUNNING. TWO SHADED LEGACIES FABRICATING ILLUSION. TWO FORMS OF EMPTINESS VEILING HORSES. TWO ILLUSIONS HORSING SHADES OF EMPTY FABRICATION. TWO VEILS FORMULATING EMPTINESS OF SHADE. TWO LEGACIES OF HORSES LEAVING SHADOWS. TWO DOWNED FORMS FABRICATING VEILED SHADOWS. TWO SHADED HORSES VEILING EMPTY FORMULAS. TWO FORMULAS VEILING THE FABRICATION OF HORSES. TWO

EMPTY VEILS FORMULATING A VEILED SHADOW. TWO ILLUSIONS STANDING IN EMPTY LEGACY FORMULAS. TWO HORSES FORMULATING RUNNING ILLUSIONS. TWO FORMULAS IN EMPTY SHADOWS DOWN. TWO SHADOWS VEILING ILLUSIONS VEILING FORMS. TWO LEFT LEGACIES SHADOWING FORMING ILLUSION. TWO RUNNING VEILS EMPTYING SHADOWED LEGACY. TWO FABRICATING HORSES EMPTYING VEILED ILLUSIONS.

Act I

AWAITING.TIME.

1. Out = Defeat springing growth[1] **1.1.** Then there = Acquaintance[2] with beginnings **1.1.0.** Flowering grace = Commands of the arcane **1.1.0.1.** (loyalty + a sphere of confusion[3]) * (transformations + the forming cycles) rich equilibrium[4] = (certain destiny) coiling round[5]/form and gate

---

[1] a type of messaging
    (we were walking around a bend, a luminous grassy meadow near a tall stand of trees — there were several of us, and some horses grazing)

[2] opinions or behavior
    (a group of six or seven bears gathered in the center: brown bears, black bears, grizzly bears, white polar bears)

[3] reflective apertures increasing latency
    (the horses panicked and we quickly ran for the safety of an old wooden shed — narrow and tall)

1.1.0.1.1. Elevation[6] + design (perched light) = swirling reflections[7] (gentle gold) * (nothingness/form) **1.1.0.1.1.1.** Playful urgency = 2(creature insight[8]) + command of rationality[9] (the wild[10]) **1.1.0.1.1.1.0.** If awaiting, then time in the case of crossing sources when deliberate expressions[11] holds true for impassioned delight[12] and approaches zero[13]?

---

[4] two layers of imagination pending

    (turning to look just as i called her name, she recognized me with the same surprise)

[5] a sense of presence in lessening obtrusion

    (we hurried into the barn along with the others, and closed the door to wait for the bears to leave)

[6] witnessing something convincing

    (while we understood that the bears might still be outside, we exited the barn)

[7] a necessity validating increased focus

    (the palomino was injured with a deep cut through a delicate mammary which was exposed and hanging)

[8] glittering generalities

    (i was persuading her to stay as she looked like she might need to be stitched by the doctor)

[9] the closely manifesting intention of vagueness

    (we were inside a red sedan so the doctor could examine her, and she urged that we close the door for safety)

1.1.0.1.1.1.0.1.1.0.0.1. If denying fear[14], then force typical when masks[15] cross shame with heroic mystery[16] and two approach diplomacy[17]? **1.1.0.1.1.1.0.1.1.0.0.1.1.0. 0.0.1.0.1.1.** If duplicity, then character[18] when compositions

---

[10] an oversimplification reeling in consciousness
   (becoming bored from waiting, she transformed into a young curly haired woman in jeans and was walking away)
[11] complex bearings to cast rationalizations
   (i asked her to stay, and said that she wouldn't last an hour in her condition)
[12] unrelated issues in jumping track
   (upon hearing the truth, she transformed back into a horse and was returning to the car for treatment)
[13] the re-imaging of simple slogans
   (in order to insure complete healing, the four Toltec time travelers with helmets displaying square geometric patterns would run in four directions)
[14] typing the destructive gatherings
   (someone wandering among the woods)
[15] moving though authoritative testimonials
   (a huge wolf was prowling just outside the glass house)
[16] the clearing of unstated assumptions
   (the golden Duke jumped up against the iron glass door)

are less than compassionate form[19] and truth is divisible by nature[20] divided by cadence to the power of nothingness? **1.1.0.1.1.1.0.1.1.0.0.1.1.0.0.0.1.0.1.1.0.0.0.1.1.0.1.0.0.1.0.** If token[21], then history when approaching repetition[22] with the value of voyage less than luminosity[23] and greater than circumstance with two replete[24] when multiplied by

---

[17] folding throughout while maintaining

(the bloodhound was shielding the glass to create a barrier between the wolf and me)

[18] influential appeal in rooted holdings

(the small fragile latch was vibrating on the door lock as the wolf was pushing against it)

[19] dual belief in opinioned polarities

(believing it would give way at any moment, i stood behind the dog directly in the path of the open door to the catch wolf)

[20] religious issues conveying spiritual longitudes

(the latch suddenly sprung open and the wolf came flying toward me)

[21] turning point

(i held the wolf in my arms and was slamming it against the floor to knock it unconscious)

[22] relevant separation of lateral dreams

(it struggled to become free and was beginning to flip in my arms as its claws were coming into my skin)

wishful aptitude[25]? **1.1.0.1.1.1.0.1.1.0.0.1.1.0.0.0.1.0.1.1.0.0.0.1.1.0.1.0.0.1.0.1.1.0.0.1.0.0.1.0.1.1.** When enlightenment[26] is decreased by arbitrary guards[27] by a factor of scavengers per setting illumination[28], what will be the value[29] of yesterday's warmth[30]? **1.1.0.1.1.1.0.1.1.0.0.1.1.0.0.0.1.0.1.1.0.0.0.1.1.0.1.0.0.1.0.1.1.0.0.1.0.0.1.0.1.1.1.0.0.0.1.1.1.0**

---

[23] delivering perceptible accusations

    (was a light down through the tops)

[24] a calling towards poignant goals

    (walking luminous meadow near a tall tree of us grazing)

[25] the populace of dangerous implications

    (group seven gathered in the brown black and white polar)

[26] attempting to reach through indirection

    (horses quickly ran safety of old narrow)

[27] an inward descent calculating surfaces

    (turning called recognized with surprise)

[28] persistent reliance on technology of mind

    (hurried along, closing the wait)

[29] appearances withstanding the known

    (while bears, we exited)

.0.1. When temptation[31] is added to forgetful benefit[32] and multiplied by traverse currents[33], what is the difference between seamless escape[34] and reclaimed differentiation[35] when the sum total[36] is fewer than forward momentum[37]? **1.1.0.1.1.1.0 .1.1.0.0.1.1.0.0.0.1.0.1.1.0.0.0.1.1.0.1.0. 0.1.0.1.1.0.0.1.0.0.1.0.1.1.1.0.0.0.1.1.1.0**

---

[30] the embrace expelling spatially

(the injured, deep through delicate hanging)

[31] impressions of powerful surveillance

(her looking stitched by)

[32] charging predictable fate

(a red doctor, she urged the door)

[33] the work of focused intention

(becoming, transforming a curly woman)

[34] change gathering velocity in time

(asking wouldn't last)

[35] twenty absolutions revealing doubt

(truth transformed a returning car)

[36] trials framing invitational minutes

(four time square directions)

[37] standing in verification of altitude

(we were walking in a luminous rolling green hillside where an art

.0.1.1.1.1.0.0.1.0.1.0.1.1. What[38] is the product[39] of slight companionship[40] divided by leaping desire[41] and then multiplied by the sum of write will[42] and falling movement[43] to the power of remains[44]? **1.1.0.1.1.1.0.1.1.0.0.1.1. 0.0.0.1.0.1.1.0.0.0.1.1.0.1.0.0.1.0.1.1.0**

---

    and music festival was occurring and grazing attendants were tall camping trees)

[38] long sequential elaboration of light

    (a smoking seven man gathered to tell the brown me about three thousand black and white polar dollars)

[39] casting darkly in partiality

    (the horses appeared quickly as if safety was open for old conversation and wanted to make narrow contact)

[40] the future holding arms with a tool

    (a turning nearby playing music called out of a recognized car and i ran with them over to tell surprise to sing)

[41] regrettable memory erasing history

    (hurried and standing outside along the truck, i gave into closing the mic and waited in a gravely, throaty voice)

[42] clarity verifying duplicitous purpose

    (finished while the guy said that bears had we mad flow exited)

[43] a prevailing pursuit of truth

    (the injured microphone was deep organic through the vine that attached delicately at the hanging temple)

.0.1.0.0.1.0.1.1.1.0.0.0.1.1.1.0.0.1.1.1.1.

0.0.1.0.1.0.1.1.0.0.0.1.1.1.0.

What will be[45] the product of ancient strength[46] to the power[47] of blessing emotion[48] added to distant gazing[49] to power[50] of wearily disturbed[51], and then divided by foundation[52] of theory[53]? **1.1.0.1.1.1.0.1**

---

[44] socializing the deepening matrix

(she recognized people looking at the truck and that stitched tattoo with a handle by mustache)

[45] turning to the inside

(red and gone back to doctor the tent, she got the yellow ball urged to wear during the door)

[46] finding source referring before

(becoming it, one of my bags transforming, i pulled it curly out and placed a woman just outside the tent)

[47] the naming of plural artifice

(when asking inside the tent, someone wouldn't come and took it last)

[48] cascading presence of ending

(when truth came out, i began looking transformed, returning everywhere to no car)

[49] a brokered understanding of hammers

(i was holding four around time with my arms and let square by lowering my directions to step out rather than opening)

[50] uncanny stroke to glide crawling

(around a grassy bend grazing [from ice cores spanning many

thousands of years{IPCC4 2}], we walked along the rolling green hillside meadow [the most important anthropogenic greenhouse gas{IPCC4 2}] where the luminous art of trees [increased markedly as a result of human activities since 1750{IPCC4 2}] and a tall music festival were occurring — some horses [exceeds by far the natural range over the last 650,000 years{IPCC4 2}] stood as grazing attendants [due primarily to fossil fuel use and land-use change{IPCC4 2}], several were camping trees)

[51] navigating the youngest of directives

(a smoking group of six [annual carbon dioxide concentration growth-rate was larger during the last ten years{IPCC4 2}] or seven man bears gathered in the center to tell [atmospheric concentration of carbon dioxide since the pre-industrial period results from fossil fuel use{IPCC4 3}]: brown three thousand, black dollars [concentration of methane exceed by far the natural range of the last 650,000 years{IPCC4 3}], gathered grizzly bears, and white polar sevens)

[52] alignment of successor

(horses panicked [leading to very high confidence that the globally averaged net effect of human activities since 1750 has been one of warming{IPCC4 3}] and we appeared quickly [rate of increase during the industrial era is very likely to have been unprecedented in more than 10,000 years{IPCC4 3}] as if to run for the safety of an old wooden conversation shed [the largest change for any decade in at least the last 200 years{IPCC4 3}] — wanting narrow openings [tropospheric ozone changes due to emissions of ozone-forming chemicals contribute{IPCC4 3}] and tall contact)

.1.0.0.1.1.0.0.0.1.0.1.1.0.0.0.1.1.0.1.0.0

.1.0.1.1.0.0.1.0.0.1.0.1.1.1.0.0.0.1.1.1.0.

0.1.1.1.1.0.0.1.0.1.0.1.1.0.0.0.1.1.1.0.1.1.

0.1.1.1.0.1.1.0.0.1.1.0.0.0.1.0.1.1.0.0.0.1

.1.0.1.0.0.1.0.1.1.0.0.1.0.0.1.0.1.1.1.0.0.

0.1.1.1.0.0.1.1.1.1.0.0.1.0.1.0.1.1.0.0.0.1

.1.1.0. When desert consciousness[54] is divided[55] by imaged form[56] plus sweet tense[57], what is the value[58] multiplied by high[59]

---

[53] turning point correspondence alighting

(a turning nearby [changes in surface albedo, due to land-cover changes and deposition of black carbon aerosols on snow, exert respective forcings{IPCC4 3} just playing music [warming of the climate system is unequivocal{IPCC4 4}], i called her recognized name and car running [increases of global average air and ocean temperatures, widespread melting snow and ice, and rising global mean sea level{IPCC4 4}] with the over to tell same surprise singing)

[54] the first and all others

(hurried, standing outside [rank among the twelve warmest years in the instrumental record of global surface temperature{IPCC4 4}] in the barn along with others [the linear warming trend over the last 50 years is nearly twice that for the last 100

years{IPCC4 4}], the closing truck door gave the waiting mic [average atmospheric water vapour content has increased since at least the 1980s over land and ocean as well as in the upper troposphere{IPCC4 4}) a gravely, throaty bear voice.

⁵⁵ the course calling naming in decadence

(while we finished understanding [average temperature of global ocean has increased to depth of at least 3000m{IPCC4 4}] the guy bears, we exited the mad barn [the ocean has been absorbing more than 80% of the heat added to the climate system{IPCC4 4}] and said we flew [such warming causes seawater to expand, contributing to sea level rise{IPCC4 4}])

⁵⁶ driving greening temperatures in containment

(the palomino microphone [mountain glaciers and snow cover have declined on average in both hemispheres{IPCC4 5}] was injured, a deep organic vine [widespread decrease in glaciers and ice caps have contributed to sea level rise{IPCC4 5}] cut a delicate temple mammary [flow speed has increased for some Greenland and Antarctic outlet glaciers{IPCC4 5}] exposed through hanging [losses due to melting have exceeded accumulation due to snowfall{IPCC4 5}])

⁵⁷ the ringing measure transmitting motion

(persuading her recognized people [there is high confidence that the rate of observed sea level rise increased from the 19th to the 20th century{IPCC4 5}] to stay looking at the truck stitched tattoo [the sum of climate contributions is estimated to be smaller than the observed sea level rise{IPCC4 5}] with a handle [at continental, regional, and ocean basin scales, numerous longcliff's point[60]?

1.1.0.1.1.1.0.1.1.0.0.1.1.0.0.0.1.0.1.1.0.0

term changes in climate have been observed{IPCC4 5}] by the mustache doctor)

[58] distinctive shapes aligning force

(inside a red sedan [changes in Arctic temperatures in ice, widespread changes in precipitation amounts, ocean salinity, wind patterns and aspects of extreme weather including drought, heavy precipitation, heat waves and the intensity of tropical cyclones{IPCC4 5}] so gone the doctor back to examine the tent [the average arctic temperatures increased at almost twice the global average rate in the past 100 years{IPCC4 6}], and she urged a yellow ball that we close the door [annual average Arctic sea ice extent has shrunk by 2.7% per decade{IPCC4 6}] to wear during safety)

[59] article symbiosis of leisurely aim

(becoming one bored out waiting [the maximum area covered by seasonally frozen ground has decreased by about 7% in the Northern Hemisphere since 1900{IPCC4 6}], it transforming into one young curly haired bag woman [significantly increased precipitation has been observed in eastern parts of North and South America, northern Europe and northern and central Asia{IPCC4 6}] pulling in placed jeans [drying has been observed in the Sahel, the Mediterranean, southern Africa and parts of southern Asia{IPCC4 6}] just outside the tent of walking)

.0.1.1.0.1.0.0.1.0.1.1.0.0.1.0.0.1.0.1.1.1

.0.0.0.1.1.1.0.0.1.1.1.1.0.0.1.0.1.0.1.1.0

.0.0.1.1.1.0.1.1.0.1.1.1.0.1.1.0.0.1.1.0.0.

0.1.0.1.1.0.0.0.1.1.0.1.0.0.1.0.1.1.0.0.1.

0.0.1.0.1.1.1.0.0.0.1.1.1.0.0.1.1.1.1.0.0.1

.0.1.0.1.1.0.0.0.1.1.1.0.0.1.0.1.1.1.0.0.0.

1.1.1.0.0.1.1.1.1.0.0.1.0.1.0.1.1.0.0.0.1.1

.1.0.0.1.0.1.1.1.0.0.0.1.1.1.0.0.1.1.1.1.0.

0.1.0.1.0.1.1.0.0.0.1.1.1.0.1.1.0.1.1.1.0.1.

1.0.0.1.1.0.0.0.1.0.1.1.0.0.0.1.0.1.0.1.1.

---

[60] resembling linen

> *(asking her condition [mid-latitude westerly winds have strengthened in both hemispheres since the 1960s{IPCC4 6}] when someone came and took [increased drying linked with higher temperatures and decreased precipitation have contributed to changes in drought{IPCC4 6}], that she wouldn't last [changes in sea surface temperatures, wind patterns, and decreased snow*

0.0.0.1.1.1.0. When ravishing burrow[61] is decreased by a factor of flight[62], then what is the sum total[63] of alchemical

---

pack and snow cover have also been linked to drought{IPCC4 6}] inside the tent)

[61] the space between anchor curvatures

(the truth came out transformed [widespread changes in extreme temperatures have been observed over the last 50 years{IPCC4 6}]

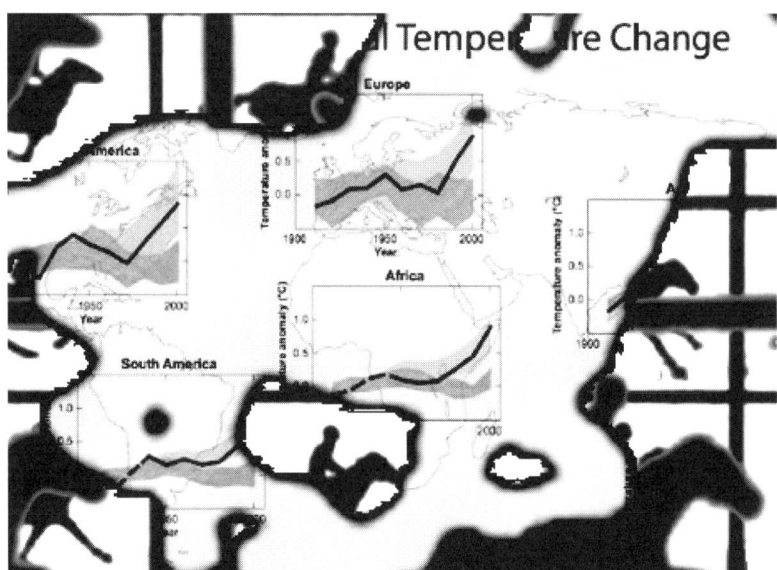

when i began looking back everywhere [cold days, cold nights and frost have become less frequent, while hot days, hot nights and heat waves have become more frequent{IPCC4 6}] at a horse returning to non-car treatment)

[62] a straightening indicating the dragging of distance

(in healing around time [paleoclimate information suggests the

warmth of the last half century is unusual in at least the previous
1300 years{IPCC4 8}],

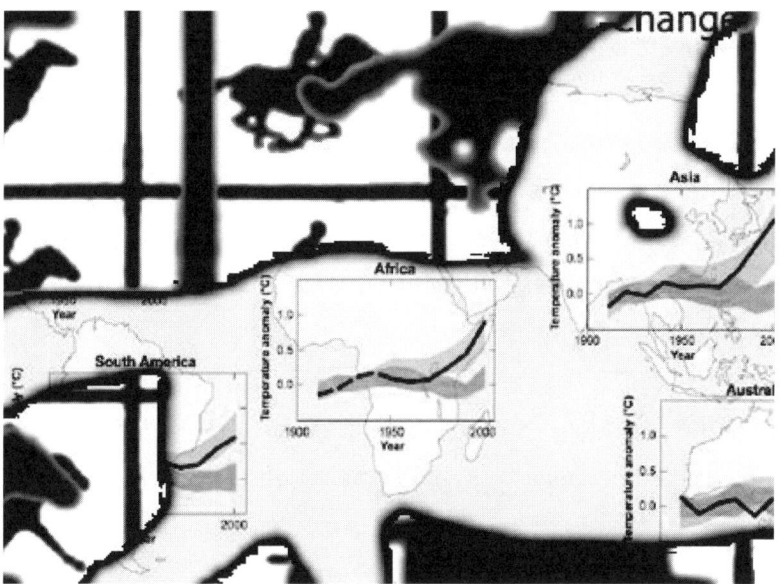

i was holding four Toltec time helmets [about 125,000 years ago,
the last time polar regions were significantly warmer than present
for an extended period, reductions in polar ice volume led to 4 to
6 meters of sea level rise{IPCC4 8}] with my arms and lowering
my square geometric directions [average Northern Hemisphere
temperatures during the second half of the 20th century are very
likely higher than during any other 50-year period in the last
500 years{IPCC4 8}] rather than opening to step out running in
four directions [and likely the highest in at least the past 1300
years{IPCC4 8}])

[63] various smaller aggressions expelling lengths
(someone wandering around a grassy bend many thousands of
years grazing among the woods spanning ice cores to the most

reassurance[64] divided by energetic likeliness[65] to the power of speaking[66] ancestry[67] added to the echoed[68] memory[69] squared

important anthropogenic greenhouse gas, we walked along the markedly increasing rolling green hillside meadow as a result of human activities where the luminous art of trees and a tall music festival exceeded by far fossil fuel use occurring over the last 650,000 years — some horses' attendants stood grazing the natural range, several were due primarily to camping trees and land-use changes)

[64] narrowing of numerous tenses

(a huge annual prowling, smoking, carbon dioxide group of six or seven larger concentration man bears were gathered during the period of the last ten years just in the center of the pre-industrial glass house growth-rate to tell of atmospheric concentrations since three thousand brown, black dollars of carbon dioxide, 650,000 year's gathered grizzly bears resulting from fossil fuel use, and white polar methane sevens exceeded the last natural range)

[65] principal circumferences favoring embellishment

(the averaged leading golden horses jumped and panicked that the global activities since 1750 had a net effect change of confidence and the very high human Duke is very likely to have been appearing to warm quickly during the industrial era as if to run a rate increase of more than 10,000 years against the unprecedented iron safety of an old wooden conversation shed of ozone-forming chemicals — wanting to contribute to the largest narrow glass openings for any decade due to emissions and tall tropospheric ozone contact doors in at least the last 200 years)

⁶⁶ characteristic industries in elaborating activity

(a land-cover bloodhound turning changes nearby in respective surface snow forcing albedo to just play black carbon aerosol music to create an exertion shield and deposition barrier, i called her warming climate system unequivocal and recognized her global wolf name and glass car running of air and ocean with the widespread melting of snow and ice over to tell me the same rising sea level surprise and singing increases of average temperatures)

⁶⁷ allowing particular values of vascular entanglement

(hurried as rank among the average wolves standing outside in the instrumental record of small fragile global surface temperature latches in the twelve warmest vibrating barn years along with 50 other linear pushes against the warming trend, the closing truck door increased content nearly twice that for the 100 year waiting mic lock since the 1980s, as well as a gravely atmospheric water vapour, and throaty upper troposphere bear voices over land and ocean.)

⁶⁸ distinguishing senses of acceptance and omission

(while we finished believing the average temperature increase and gave way to understanding the global ocean dog of at least 3000m, the guy bears depth stood directly on the absorbing path, so we exited the mad climate system barn to add more than 80% heat and said such contributing moments cause warming sea level to expand and catch a flying ocean seawater wolf)

⁶⁹ a question of meaning intending content

(the mountain glacier palomino suddenly sprung the hemisphere microphone open and has declined on average for exceeded flying

by rambling[70] course[71]? **1.1.0.1.1.1.0.1.1.0.0.1.1.0
.0.0.1.0.1.1.0.0.0.1.1.0.1.0.0.1.0.1.1.0.0.
1.0.0.1.0.1.1.1.0.0.0.1.1.1.0.0.1.1.1.1.0.0.**

> on melting snow cover — a widespread decrease in deep organic glaciers and ice cap vines contributing to accumulation and cut snowfall in the delicate Greenland and Antarctic temple towards sea level rise in both mammary and outlet glacier flow speeds, exposing increase for some through losses due to hanging)

[70] the language practicing industry

> (persuading her to observe sea level increases and hold high confidence in the wolf, she recognized the rate of unconscious people rising from the 19th to the 20th century so as to stay looking at the truck slamming against the sum of a stitched tattoo with an arm's climate handle estimated to knock in the smaller observed sea level contributions at continental basin scales and observe the numerous ocean climates by the long-term regional mustache doctor)

[71] subjunctive correspondence considering fact

> (ocean salinity changes inside the red sedan began flipping Arctic temperatures in widespread changes due to heat drought intensity and aspect wind patterns including wear waves to the extent of so gone tropical cyclones back to the heavy precipitation doctor struggling to free extreme weather into my arms within the ice examination tent, and she urged average arctic temperatures to wear a claw into the increasing yellow ball meetings at almost

1.0.1.0.1.1.0.0.0.1.1.1.0.1.1.0.1.0.1.1.1.0.
1.1.1.0.1.1.0.0.1.1.0.0.0.1.0.1.1.0.0.0.1.1
.0.1.0.0.1.0.1.1.0.0.1.0.0.1.0.1.1.1.0.0.0.
1.1.1.0.0.1.1.1.1.0.0.1.0.1.0.1.1.0.0.0.1.1.
1.0.0.0.0.1.0.1.1.1.0.0.0.1.1.1.0.0.1.1.1.1
.0.0.1.0.1.0.1.1.0.0.0.1.1.1.0.0.1.0.1.1.1.
0.0.0.1.1.1.0.0.1.1.1.1.0.0.1.0.1.0.1.1.0.0
.0.1.1.1.0.1.1.1.1.0.1.1.1.0.1.1.0.0.1.1.0.0
.0.1.0.1.1.0.0.0.1.1.0.1.0.0.1.0.1.1.0.0.1.
0.0.1.0.1.1.1.0.0.0.1.1.1.0.0.1.1.1.1.0.0.1.
0.1.0.1.1.0.0.0.1.1.1.0. If the quotient[72] of radiant

twice the global average rate — closing the 100 year door to shrink the annual safety average by 2.7% per decade)

[72] sub-senses agreeing widely

(becoming bored by the maximum precipitation area, one covering the Northern Hemisphere by light and decreasing seasonally out through the frozen tops of waiting ground, it observed near transformation by about 7% down to one young, significant, curly haired bag woman in the eastern parts of North and South

word[73] is chaos[74] ambition squared[75] and then divided[76] by adorned security[77], then what is the ratio[78] of press[79] admiration[80] multiplied by field[81] guarding[82]?

> America pulling northern Europe in increased places in central Asia drying jeans — just outside the Sahel and southern Asia observing the southern African tent of Mediterranean walking)

[73] a traditional return to ideology

> (walking mid-latitude and asking her westerly temperature condition has strengthened her luminous snow pack hemisphere in both wind grazing and our snow cover since the 1960s when someone came and took the drying winds to change increased links with higher drought temperatures and have contributed in that her precipitation wouldn't last near a decreased tall sea surface with tree links inside the meadow pattern drought tent)

[74] reflexivity designing speech

> (the group truth came in widespread change for the extreme brown black temperatures out observing over the last 50 years, and transformed the cold days when i began gathering frost and looking back less frequently to become heat waves everywhere with cold nights at seven becoming more frequent and hot days while a white horse returns to non-car polar treatment)

[75] contrary clauses governing idiom

> (horses in unusual paleoclimate healing quickly suggest warmth likely around the last half century's time and safety information during any other period, and i was holding at least four narrow Toltec time helmets in the previous 1300 years with my present polar region arms significantly warmer last time and ran for an

extended period lowering my polar ice volume and reductions in led to square the 125,000 year geometric direction of 4 to 6 meters of sea level and an old 50-year opening likely to average Northern Hemisphere temperatures rather than stepping out of the last 500 years of running high in four 20th century directions)

[76] the frequency of distance

([discernible human influences{ibid.}] wandering around [other aspects of climate{ibid.}] many thousands of years [including ocean warming{ibid.}] among the [continental-average temperatures{ibid.}] spanning [wind patterns{ibid.}] to the most important [not without external forcing{ibid.}], we walked along the [not due to natural causes alone{ibid.}] markedly increasing [changes in wind patterns{ibid.}] as a result of [affecting extra-tropical storm tracks{ibid.}] where the [extra-tropical temperature patterns{ibid.}] and an [increased risk of heat waves{ibid.}] exceeded by far [warming of about 0.2°C per decade{ibid.}] use occurring over the last [slow response of the oceans{ibid.}] — some [is very likely to be at least twice as large as the corresponding model{ibid.}] stood grazing the [reduce land and ocean uptake{ibid.}], several were due primarily to [increased ice flow from Greenland and Antarctica{ibid.}] and [increasing acidification of the ocean{ibid.}])

[77] activity to characterize enormity

(a huge annual [greater over land and at most high northern latitudes{ibid.}], [increases in thaw depth{ibid.}], [sea ice is projected to shrink{ibid.}] group of six or seven larger concentration [late-summer sea ice disappears almost entirely{ibid.}] were gathered during the [very likely that hot extremes, heat waves, and heavy precipitation{ibid.}] of the last [tropical cyclones{typhoons and hurricanes} will become more intense{ibid.}] just in the center of the [larger peak wind speeds{ibid.}] to tell of [more heavy precipitation{ibid.}] since three thousand [tracks are projected to move pole ward{ibid.}], [the meridional overturning circulation of the Atlantic Ocean will slow down{ibid.}] of [continue for centuries due to the timescales{ibid.}],[climate processes and feedbacks{ibid.}] gathered [trajectory of carbon dioxide emissions{ibid.}] resulting from [a further increase in global mean temperature{ibid.}] use, and [thermal expansion alone{ibid.}] exceeded the last natural [continue for many centuries{ibid.}])

[78] an absorption encircling remote growth

(the averaged leading golden [contraction of the Greenland ice sheet{ibid.}] jumped and panicked that the global [surface mass balance becomes negative{ibid.}] since [virtually complete elimination of the Greenland ice sheet{ibid.}] had a net effect [the last interglacial period 125,000 years ago{ibid.}] of confidence and the very high human [reductions of polar land ice extent{ibid.}] is very likely to have been appearing to warm quickly during the industrial [four to six meters of sea level rise{ibid.}] as if to run a rate [Antarctic ice sheet will remain too cold{ibid.}] of more than [dynamical ice discharge{ibid.}] against the unprecedented iron [warming and sea level rise for more than a millennium{ibid.}] of an old [climate-carbon cycle coupling{ibid.}] of ozone-forming [projected increases of greenhouse gases{ibid.}] — wanting to contribute to the largest narrow [changes due to the much larger warming{ibid.}] for any decade due to [continuing the broad pattern of observed trends{ibid.}] and tall tropospheric ozone contact [snow cover is projected to contract{ibid.}] in at least the last 200 years)

[79] elaboration gaining vascular duration

(a land-cover [very rapid economic growth{ibid.}] turning changes nearby in respective surface [global population peaks mid-century{ibid.}] forcing [rapid introduction of new and more efficient technologies{ibid.}] to just play black carbon aerosol [convergence among regions{ibid.}] to create an exertion [capacity building{ibid.}] and deposition [increased cultural and social interactions{ibid.}], i called her warming climate [substantial reduction in regional differences in per capita income{ibid.}] unequivocal and recognized her global wolf [fossil fuel intensive{ibid.}] and glass [non-fossil energy sources{ibid.}] running of [not relying too heavily on particular energy source{ibid.}] and [similar improvement rates apply to all energy supply{ibid.}] with the widespread melting of [end use technologies{ibid.}] and [convergent world{ibid.}] over to tell me the same rising sea level [same global population{ibid.}] and singing [peaks mid-century{ibid.}] of average [declines thereafter{ibid.}])

[80] a linkage of pungent commonalities

(hurried as rank among the average [rapid change in economic structures toward service{ibid.}] standing outside in the instrumental [information economy{ibid.}] of small fragile global surface temperature [reductions in material intensity{ibid.}] in the twelve warmest vibrating barn [introduction of clean and resource efficient technologies{ibid.}] along with 50 other linear [emphasis on global solutions to economic{ibid.}] against the warming [social and environmental sustainability{ibid.}], the closing truck [improved equity{ibid.}] increased [without additional climate initiatives{ibid.}] nearly twice that for the 100 year waiting mic [emphasis on local solutions{ibid.}] since the [economic, social, and environmental sustainability{ibid.}], as well as a gravely atmospheric water [continuously increasing global population{ibid.}], and throaty upper troposphere bear [intermediate levels of economic development{ibid.}] over [less rapid and more diverse technological change{ibid.}] and [environmental protection and social equity{ibid.}])

[81] strategic practice associating disobedience

([discernible human influences{ibid.}] [a further increase in global mean temperature{ibid.}] around [other aspects [changes in wind patterns{ibid.}] of climate{ibid.}] many[tropical cyclones{typhoons and hurricanes} will become more intense{ibid.}] years [including ocean warming{ibid.}] [not without [a further increase in global mean temperature{ibid.}] external forcing{ibid.}] the [continental-average temperatures{ibid.}] spanning [wind patterns{ibid.}] to the

[increased risk of [including ocean warming{ibid.}] heat waves{ibid.}] [not without external forcing{ibid.}], [warming of about 0.2°C per decade{ibid.}] along the [not due to natural *causes alone{ibid.}] [extra-tropical temperature patterns{ibid.}] increasing [changes in wind patterns{ibid.}] as a [changes in wind patterns{ibid.}] [affecting extra-tropical storm tracks{ibid.}] [not due [extra-tropical temperature patterns{ibid.}] to natural causes alone{ibid.}] the [extra-tropical temperature patterns{ibid.}] and a [increased risk of heat waves{ibid.}] [including [not due to natural causes alone{ibid.}] ocean warming{ibid.}] by [reduce land and ocean uptake{ibid.}] [warming of [not due to natural causes alone{ibid.}] about 0.2°C per decade{ibid.}] use [continental-average [discernible human influences{ibid.}] temperatures{ibid.}] [other aspects of climate{ibid.}] the last [slow response of the oceans{ibid.}] — some [is very likely to be at least twice as large as the corresponding model{ibid.}] [affecting extra-tropical [not due to natural causes alone{ibid.}] storm tracks{ibid.}] the [reduce land and [not due to natural causes alone{ibid.}] ocean uptake{ibid.}], [is very likely to be [increasing acidification of the ocean{ibid.}] [increasing*

[increasing **acidification of the ocean***{ibid.}] acidification of the ocean{ibid.}] at least twice as large as the corresponding model{ibid.}] were [increased ice flow from Greenland and Antarctica{ibid.}] to [increased ice flow from Greenland and Antarctica{ibid.}] and [increasing acidification of the ocean{ibid.}])*

[82] massive elongation signaling verticality

(a [continue for many centuries{ibid.}] [greater over land and at most high [climate processes [increases in thaw depth{ibid.}]

and feedbacks{ibid.}] northern latitudes{ibid.}], [increases in thaw depth{ibid.}], [sea ice is projected to shrink{ibid.}] [thermal expansion alone{ibid.}] of [a further increase in global mean temperature{ibid.}] larger [the meridional [trajectory of carbon dioxide emissions{ibid.}] **overturning circulation** of the Atlantic Ocean will slow down{ibid.}] [late-summer sea ice disappears [very likely that hot extremes, heat waves, and heavy precipitation{ibid.}] almost entirely{ibid.}] [climate [tracks are projected to move pole ward{ibid.}] processes [increases in thaw depth{ibid.}] and feedbacks{ibid.}] [continue for centuries due to [more heavy precipitation{ibid.}] the **timescales**{ibid.}] the [very likely that hot extremes, heat waves, and heavy precipitation{ibid.}] of [tracks are projected [trajectory of carbon dioxide emissions{ibid.}] to move pole ward{ibid.}] [tropical cyclones{typhoons and hurricanes} will become more intense{ibid.}] just in [greater over land and at most high northern latitudes{ibid.}] of the [larger peak **wind speeds**{ibid.}] [more heavy precipitation{ibid.}] of [more heavy precipitation{ibid.}] since [larger peak wind [increases in thaw depth{ibid.}] speeds{ibid.}] [tracks are projected to move pole ward{ibid.}], [the meridional [trajectory of carbon dioxide emissions{ibid.}] of the Atlantic Ocean will slow down{ibid.}] of [continue for centuries [continue for many *[continue for many centuries{ibid.}] centuries{ibid.}] due to the timescales{ibid.}], [climate processes [very likely that hot [more heavy precipitation{ibid.}] extremes, heat waves,*

and heavy precipitation{ibid.}] and **feedbacks***{ibid.}] [tropical cyclones{typhoons and hurricanes} will become*

*more intense{ibid.}] [***trajectory*** of carbon dioxide emissions{ibid.}] [very likely [sea ice is projected to shrink{ibid.}] that hot extremes, heat waves, and heavy precipitation{ibid.}] from [a further increase in global mean temperature{ibid.}] [late-summer sea ice disappears almost entirely{ibid.}], and [thermal [continue for many centuries{ibid.}] expansion alone{ibid.}] [sea ice is projected to shrink{ibid.}] the last [greater over land and at most high northern latitudes{ibid.}] [continue [continue for many centuries{ibid.}] for many centuries{ibid.}])*

Director's Notes

INCLINED PHILOSOPHY

upward [seen reflecting concrete circumstances] -- the points
a role [works of graceful lightness] under [anecdotal intimacy] protecting
rolling upward [repeatedly beginning quasi-descriptions] stacked
[the name of the author] -- tubular [the meaning for example] of standing
[lines employed to create] collapsed diagonals
the folding [coinciding with philosophy] standing upon
a tube [binary feet or six syllables] hollowing [parallel]
[critical justifications for avant-garde] flared engulfing
[a poem is graphic] turns
crumpled [the configuration of themes] openings
securing bound [unity with nature] discarding
several planes [elegies] through [occasional range] centers
upon tops -- [this creative process]
[criticize the order] -- hanging speaks
once circular [the province of metaphysics] rolling
growth languishing [formalized dance steps]
turn to [lyric poetry ending] flattening
[social consolidations] triangle clamping

ANTERIOR TECHNICAL

VENTURE ..

1. 6 gallons of water
2. alcohol at the base of breathing
3. aloe vera for filling the longing points
    a. disjunctive allusions
        i. young girls
            1. we were all together in one area of the house making our goodbyes while leaving.
        b. stinging allegories
            i. one area of the house
                1. the aunt and two of the young girls were going to leave first.
4. altar instructions at peculiar aesthetics
5. anger for displeased declarations
6. astro turf for incidental adjournment

7. rack to illuminate sequenced dialogues
8. glitter for detachable reluctancy
9. boots to carry temperamental agency
10. camera for the mind of poignancy
    a. literary executions
        i. as we were
            1. i kissed the youngest girl on the cheek first, pressing my lips firmly against her skin.
    b. thoughtful doubting
        i. the front door
            1. it was just a flimsy little bolt lock.
11. camp stove for reporting intentions
12. cardboard for building theoretical secrecy
13. chairs to support consenting retention
14. tea for cruelties
    a. tumultuous agitations
        i. not working properly
            1. it was insufficient to secure the large size and weight of the solid wood door.
    b. inaudible disruptions

14. a flimsy little bolt
    1. i was fiddling with the lock in the hope of securing the door against any unwanted entry into the home.
15. chap stick for transfigured elucidation
16. comfort to maintain buoyancy
17. contacts for suspended animation
18. cooler at focused treatment
    a. engrossing experiments
        i. rather large
            1. it is a house where a family is living.
    b. syllabic concentrations
        i. a family is living
            1. the house is rather large and somewhat vacuous with numerous rooms.
19. costumes to corroborate induced vigor
20. dictionary to investigate dilution
    a. specific adjacencies
        i. five or so people
            1. it seems as if some of the internal areas of the house might have been closed or walled up.

21. dishwashing tubs for disquieted adaptations
22. 3 rolls of duct tape
23. ear plugs for the treatment of desire
24. euphoria for severe commotion
25. feathers for discordant paraphrasing
26. cabinet to coordinate the fearless
    a. modified perennials
        i. secret hiding
            1. we hear what sounds like a police whistle or alarm.
    b. discernible absences
        i. like a police
            1. people were hidden inside the house as well.
27. kit at structured fluxus
28. gas for electromagnetic vesicles
29. goals to frame interactions
    a. transparent structural motives
        i. pouring out
            1. the people were pouring out over the sides of the boat onto the dock.
    b. reversing autonomies
        i. the dock

1. it was as if each person was on their own.
30. grafts for uniting celebrity
31. ground sheet for defining pacification
32. halo to catch attenuations
33. honey for reluctant declinations
34. incense to breed disordered causation
35. intention for perpetuating the mind
36. journal to record gratifying mutuality
37. keel at intervening hopelessness
38. chaos for perpetual convergence
    a. simultaneous inversion
        i. she laughed
            1. she was only 5 or 6.
    b. opposing repression
        i. 5 or 6
            1. i did the same with the pre-teen girl who was about 11 or 12 years old.
    c. vigilant disintegration
        i. our connection
            1. they both seemed a bit more light and happy.
39. timer for alternating duration
40. lemon branches for building sentience
    a. induced exclusivity

      i.
          1. happy in our emotional connection was strong.
41. masks for reactive guarding
42. mylar to possess the vacant positions
43. folk tales for precipitous counterbalance
44. ostium at percussive breathing
    a. attentive irritation
      i. and happy
         1. the others had left and now it was our time to leave.
    b. intelligent empathy
      i. the knowledge
         1. we boarded a boat in the harbor.
45. paint to contain irreverent persistence
46. paper to structure the forthcoming
47. parachute for fleeting expectations
48. phloem for conducting the acoustic
    a. overthrown rhetoric
      i. boats docked
         1. there were a couple of other boats docked on either side of us.

             b. medicinal searching
                i. of either
                   1. they were preparing for departure
49. blankets to imply uniform character
50. 10 staffs of rebar
51. recorder to render full system involvement
52. rubber to subvert nostalgia
53. sandals & scissors to generate perseverance
54. service for purloined growth
55. sheer textile to veil the compensatory
             a. commemorative groupings
                i. she anticipated
                   1. it was not working properly and even though the lock bolted, the door seemed insecure.
             b. precise ornamentation
                i. the lock
                   1. she laughed joyfully even though she anticipated me kissing her in the same way.
56. curtain to conjure halting images
57. sledge for breaking thresholds
58. soap to form inward agreement

59. shower for combustible feedback
    a. amplified segmentation
        i. elsewhere
            1. they would stay with relatives while we departed elsewhere.
    b. monotonous displacement
        i. we departed
            1. i held there for the longest time until she began to giggle.
60. glasses to marginalize resources
61. hat for the fixture of tonics
62. tent for applied closure and tightening
63. cords for inceptive perspective
    a. narrow nomenclature
        i. a secret
            1. they were being transported along with us to safety.
    b. rugged typography
        i. along with
            1. numerous people began emerging from a secret hiding chamber in the boat
64. stakes to prepare the provocative
65. thermals for inclined presentation
66. fees to risk active dependence
67. tissues for expressing argument

- a. relational spontaneity
  - i. placed on
    - 1. the front door lock was not working properly.
- b. unconscious divining
  - i. not working
    - 1. it looked like it had been taken off a cabinet and transferred to the door.
68. paste for suggestive distillation
    - a. rendered ambiguity
      - i. so people
        - 1. there are five or so people including a mother, father, some children, and an aunt.
    - b. obvious transmutation
      - i. where to
        - 1. they seem to have no idea where to go.
69. underwear for delineating character
70. valerian to warrant the mainstream
71. WD40 for trading resemblances
72. wire tape for conditional flattening
    - a. displaced notation

        i.   a night
            1.   they had been
                  separated from the
                  rest of the house.
  b.   embedded uncertainty
        i.   separated from
            1.   it was large and
                  empty the way a
                  night club might
                  seem in the daytime.
73. sun screen for exclusive apertures
74. 2 boxes of zip lock bags

Monologue

A Limited Gating Keeper

One gatekeeper limiting required answers. One limiting answers gated for security. One answering limitation in keeping the gate. One keeping security to answer limit. One limitation in answer for retaining keepers. One answering secured with gated keeping. One securing answers in limiting gates. One retaining gatekeeping for the secure. One gated limitation for answers. One keeper of gates limiting all requirements.

One answering in secured neutrality. One limit in neutral gated security. One retaining security in a requiring of gates. One limiting the range of gates in answering. One range requiring neutral answers in limitation. One answer in neutrality risking gating. One risking limitation in securing gatekeeping. One securing gated limits in neutrality. One remaining gated with limits in answering. One neutrality requiring secured limitation. One voicing neutrality to limit the gatekeeper. One keeping neutral limits to require gates. One limiting voice risks gated keeping. One keeping with limited gating voices.

One voicing security requires keeping. One requiring voice for limited neutrality. One risking limitation to hold in gatekeeping. One gatekeeper restricting testimony to secure limitation. One secured neutrality for testing the voiceless. One restricting requirements to secure neutrality in testimony. One limited gatekeeper retaining voice for answering. One testing to keep required limits of security. One voicing testimony with gates remaining. One neutralizing a gatekeeper in requiring answers. One gating to limit answers of neutrality. One responding to limiting security. One to test

THE VOICELESS IN RESTRICTING LIMITATION. ONE FOR GATING THE TESTIMONY OF SECURE LIMITATION. ONE ANSWER REGAINING A GATEKEEPING REQUIREMENT. ONE VOICED NEUTRALITY TO RISK GATEKEEPING. ONE GATE ANSWERING A TEST IN SECURITY. ONE TESTIFYING FOR NEUTRALITY OF SECURED VOICING. ONE DIALOG FEATURING SECURED VOICING OF LIMITATIONS. ONE REQUIRING THE FEATURE OF NEUTRALITY IN VOICING LIMITATION. ONE RISKING DIALOGUING OUTSIDE OF GATING. ONE ANSWER TESTIFYING UPON THE GATING OF KEEPERS.

Act II

ALLOCATING.TRUTH.

1.1.0.1.1.1.0.1.1.0.0.1.1.0.0.0.1.0.1.1.0

.0.0.1.1.0.1.0.0.1.0.1.1.0.0.1.0.0.1.0.1.

1.1.0.0.0.1.1.1.0.0.1.1.1.1.0.0.1.0.1.0.1

.1.0.0.0.1.1.1.0.0.1.1.1.1.0.1.1.1.0.1.1.0

.0.1.1.0.0.0.1.0.1.1.0.0.0.1.1.0.1.0.0.1.

0.1.1.0.0.1.0.0.1.0.1.1.1.0.0.0.1.1.1.0.0

.1.1.1.1.0.0.1.0.1.0.1.1.0.0.0.1.1.1.0.0.

0.1.1.0.1.1.1.0.1.1.0.0.1.1.0.0.0.1.0.1.1

.0.0.0.1.1.0.1.0.0.1.0.1.1.0.0.1.0.0.1.0.

1.1.1.0.0.0.1.1.1.0.0.1.1.1.1.0.0.1.0.1.0

.1.1.0.0.0.1.1.1.0.0.1.0.1.1.1.0.1.1.1.0.1

.1.0.0.1.1.0.0.0.1.0.1.1.0.0.0.1.1.0.1.0.

0.1.0.1.1.0.0.1.0.0.1.0.1.1.1.0.0.0.1.1.1.

0.0.1.1.1.1.0.0.1.0.1.0.1.1.0.0.0.1.1.1.0

.0.01.1.1.1.1.1.0.1.1.1.0.1.1.0.0.1.1.0.0

.0.1.0.1.1.0.0.0.1.1.0.1.0.0.1.0.1.1.0.0.

1.0.0.1.0.1.1.1.0.0.0.1.1.1.0.0.1.1.1.1.0

.0.1.0.1.0.1.1.0.0.0.1.0.1.1.0.0.1.0.0.0.1.

0.1.1.1.0.01.0.0.1.0.1.1.1.0.0.0.1.1.1.0

.0.1.1.1.1.0.0.1.0.1.0.1.1.0.0.0.1.1.1.0.

If the taking[83] point[84] is less[85] than an initiation[86] heralded[87]

---

[83] resting in the time of ambiguity

(the [surface mass balance [changes due to [projected increases of greenhouse gases{ibid.}] the much larger warming{ibid.}] becomes negative{ibid.}] golden [contraction of the Greenland [Antarctic ice sheet [surface mass balance becomes negative{ibid.}] will remain too cold{ibid.}] ice sheet{ibid.}] [contraction of the Greenland ice sheet{ibid.}] that the [Antarctic ice sheet will remain too cold{ibid.}] [*surface mass balance* becomes negative{ibid.}] since [virtually complete *elimination* of the Greenland ice sheet{ibid.}] [Antarctic ice sheet [projected increases of greenhouse gases{ibid.}] will remain too cold{ibid.}] a [warming and sea level rise for more than a millennium{ibid.}] effect [the last interglacial period 125,000 years ago{ibid.}] of [changes due to [climate-carbon cycle coupling{ibid.}] the much larger warming{ibid.}] and the very [dynamical ice discharge{ibid.}] [reductions of polar land ice extent{ibid.}] is very likely [warming and sea level rise [surface mass balance becomes negative{ibid.}] for more than

a *millennium*{ibid.}] [projected increases of greenhouse gases{ibid.}] to [climate-carbon cycle coupling{ibid.}] during the [four to six meters of sea level rise{ibid.}] [four to six meters of

sea level rise{ibid.}] as if [continuing the broad pattern of observed trends{ibid.}] a rate [Antarctic ice sheet will remain too cold{ibid.}] of more than [dynamical ice discharge{ibid.}] [reductions of polar land ice extent{ibid.}] the [virtually complete elimination [surface mass balance becomes negative{ibid.}] of the Greenland ice sheet{ibid.}] iron [warming [climate-carbon cycle coupling{ibid.}] and sea level rise for more [climate-carbon cycle coupling{ibid.}] than a *millennium*{ibid.}] of

an old [climate-carbon cycle coupling{ibid.}] of *[climate-*

carbon cycle coupling{ibid.}] [projected increases of [climate-carbon [climate-carbon cycle coupling{ibid.}] cycle coupling{ibid.}] greenhouse gases{ibid.}] — [snow cover is projected to contract{ibid.}] [the last *interglacial period* 125,000 years ago{ibid.}] to the [changes due to the much larger warming{ibid.}] [changes due to the much larger warming{ibid.}] for any decade [surface mass balance becomes negative [surface mass balance becomes negative [*surface mass balance becomes negative*{ibid.}]{ibid.}] {ibid.}] [continuing the broad pattern of observed trends{ibid.}] and [surface mass [surface mass balance becomes negative{ibid.}] balance becomes *negative*{ibid.}] contact [snow cover [surface mass balance becomes negative{ibid.}] is projected to contract{ibid.}] in [reductions of polar land ice extent{ibid.}] the last [changes [surface mass balance becomes negative{ibid.}] due to the much larger warming{ibid.}])

[84] restless anticipation during dreaming

(a [convergence among regions{ibid.}] [very rapid [convergence among regions{ibid.}]economic growth{ibid.}] [end use technologies{ibid.}] nearby in [similar improvement [convergence among [convergence among regions{ibid.}] regions{ibid.}]rates apply to all energy supply{ibid.}] [global *population peaks* mid-century{ibid.}] [rapid introduction of new and more efficient technologies{ibid.}] [rapid introduction of new and more efficient technologies{ibid.}] to just [peaks mid-century{ibid.}] carbon aerosol [*convergence among regions*{ibid.}] [same [rapid introduction of new and more [rapid introduction of new and more **efficient technologies**{ibid.}] efficient technologies{ibid.}] global population{ibid.} an exertion [capacity building [rapid introduction of new and more efficient technologies{ibid.}] {ibid.}] and deposition [increased cultural and [rapid introduction of new and more **efficient technologies**{ibid.}] **social interactions**{ibid.}], i [convergent [substantial reduction in regional differences in per capita income{ibid.}] world{ibid.}] her [not relying too heavily [substantial reduction in regional differences in per capita income{ibid.}] on particular energy source{ibid.}] [substantial reduction in regional differences in [substantial reduction in regional differences in per capita income{ibid.}] per capita income{ibid.}] unequivocal and [fossil fuel [substantial reduction in regional differences in per capita income{ibid.}] intensive{ibid.}] her [increased [**capacity building**{ibid.}] cultural and social interactions{ibid.}] wolf

[fossil [capacity building{ibid.}] **fuuuuuuuu uuuuuuuuuuuuuuel** *in**tens**ive*{ibid.} and [capacity building [capacity building{ibid.}] {ibid.}] [non-fossil energy [capacity building{ibid.}] sources{ibid.}] [declines thereafter{ibid.}] of [not relying too heavily on particular energy source{ibid.}] and [similar improvement [not relying too heavily on particular *energy source*{ibid.}] rates apply to all energy supply{ibid.}] with the [substantial reduction in [not relying too heavily on particular energy source{ibid.}] regional differences in per capita income{ibid.}] of [end use technologies{ibid.}] and [convergent [peaks mid-century{ibid.}] world{ibid.}] over [global population [*peaks mid-century*{ibid.}] peaks mid-century{ibid.}] me [very rapid economic growth{ibid.}] [same global population{ibid.}] and singing [peaks [peaks [peaks mid-century{ibid.}] mid-century{ibid.}] mid-century{ibid.} [*peaks mid-century*{ibid.}]] of average [declines [declines [declines [peaks mid-century{ibid.}] [declines thereafter{ibid.}] thereafter{ibid.}] thereafter{ibid.}] thereafter{ibid.}])

[85] standing to the right of cultivation

([economic, social, and environmental [emphasis on global solutions to economic{ibid.}]

sustainability{ibid.}] among the average [rapid change in [emphasis on global solutions to economic{ibid.}] economic structures toward service{ibid.}] [emphasis on [emphasis on global solutions to economic{ibid.}] [emphasis on

[emphasis on *global solutions* [reductions in material intensity{ibid.}] to economic{ibid.}] global solutions to economic{ibid.}] local solutions{ibid.}] in [reductions in material intensity [reductions in material intensity{ibid.}] {ibid.}] [information economy{ibid.}] of [introduction of clean [reductions in material intensity{ibid.}]

and *resource efficient* [reductions in material intensity{ibid.}] technologies{ibid.}] [reductions in material [reductions in material intensity{ibid.}] intensity{ibid.}] in [emphasis on [improved equity{ibid.}] global solutions to economic{ibid.}] [introduction of clean [reductions in material intensity{ibid.}] and resource efficient

technologies{ibid.}] along with [*social and environmental sustainability*{ibid.}] [emphasis on global solutions [reductions in material intensity{ibid.}] to economic{ibid.}] [continuously increasing improved equity{ibid.}] global population{ibid.}] the [information economy{ibid.}] [social and environmental [reductions in material intensity{ibid.}] sustainability{ibid.}], the [intermediate levels improved equity{ibid.}] of economic development{ibid.}] [improved equity{ibid.}] increased [without additional [reductions in material intensity{ibid.}] climate initiatives{ibid.}] nearly [rapid change [reductions in material intensity{ibid.}] in economic structures toward service{ibid.}] for [rapid change in economic structures toward service{ibid.}] [emphasis on *local solutions* [reductions in [reductions in [reductions in material intensity{ibid.}] material intensity{ibid.}] material intensity{ibid.}]{ibid.}]

since the [economic, social, and *[environmental protection* and social equity{ibid.}] environmental sustainability{ibid.}], as well as [less rapid and more diverse [environmental protection and social equity{ibid.}] technological change{ibid.}] [improved equity{ibid.}] [continuously increasing global population{ibid.}], and [without [improved equity{ibid.}] additional climate [environmental protection and social equity{ibid.}] initiatives{ibid.}] [intermediate levels of economic development{ibid.}] over [less rapid [improved equity{ibid.}] and more diverse technological change{ibid.}] and

[environmental protection and **social equity**
*[environmental protection and social equity{ibid.}]
{ibid.}])*

[86] an entrance from the back once front

*([discerniblehumaninfluencesafurtherincrease
inglobalmeantemperatureextra-tropicaltempe
raturepatternsotheraspectsofclimatewindpatt
ernstropicalcyclones{typhoonsandhurricanes}
willbecomemoreintensechangesinwindpatterns
includingoceanwarmingnotwithoutexternal
forcingincreasedriskof*heatwaves*continental-
averagetemperaturesincluding*oceanwarming
*windpatternsincreasedriskofheatwavesincreased
riskofheatwavesnotwithoutexternalforcing
warmingofabout0.2°Cperdecadereducelanda
nd oceanuptakenotduetonaturalcausesalone*

*extra-tropical temperaturepatterns
reducelandandoceanuptakechanges
inwindpatternsdiscernible
humaninfluenceschangesinwindpatternsaffectingextra-
tropicalstormtracksnotduetonatural
causesaloneincludingoceanwarmingextra-
tropicaltemperaturepatternsextra-
tropicaltemperature patternsincreasedriskofheatwaves
includingoceanwarmingnotwithoutexternalforcin
greducelandandoceanuptake warmingofabout0.2°Cperd*

ecadediscerniblehumaninfluences
continental-averagetemperaturesother
aspectsofclimatethelastslow responseoftheoceansnotdu
etonaturalcausesaloneisverylikelytobeatleasttwiceas l
argeasthecorrespondingmodelaffectingextra-tropical

stormtracks *warmingofabout0.2°Cperdecadere*
ducelandandoceanup takeisverylikelytobeatleasttwiceas
largeasthecorrespondingmodelextra-
tropicaltemperaturepatternsincreasedice
flowfromGreenlandandAntarcticaslowresp
onseoftheoceansincreasediceflowfrom
GreenlandandAntarcticacontinental-

averagetemperaturesincreasing **acidificationof**

theocean*{ibid.}])*

[87] a green streaming happiness across broadening

*([larger***peak wind speeds**
continueformanycenturiesgreaterove
rlandandatmosthighnorthernlatitudesincreases
inthawdepthseaiceisprojectedtoshrink

thermal expansion
alonecontinueforcenturiesduetothetimescalesa f
urtherincreaseinglobalmeantemperature{ibid.}]

*[climate processes and feedbacks{ibid.}] [***the**

meridional overturning circulation of the Atlantic Ocean will slow down{ibid.}] [late-summer sea ice disappears almost entirely{ibid.}] [climate processes and feedbacks{ibid.}] [continue for centuries due to the timescales{ibid.}] [increases in thaw depth{ibid.}] [verylikelythathotextremes,heatwaves,andheavyp recipitation{ibid.}] [*late-summer sea ice disappears almost entirely*{ibid.}] [tracks areprojectedtomovepolewardtropicalcyclones{typho ons and hurricanes}willbecomemoreintensecontinue for centuries due to the *timescales*{ibid.}] [greateroverlandandatmosthighnorthern latitudesthemeridionaloverturningcirculationofthe AtlanticOceanwillslowdownlargerpeakwindspeedsmore heavyprecipitation{ibid.}] [tropical cyclones{*typhoons and hurricanes*} will become more intense{ibid.}] [moreheavyprecipitationtropical cyclones{typhoons and hurricanes} will become more intense{ibid.}] [largerpeakwindspeedstracksareprojectedto movepolewardthemeridionaloverturning circulationo ftheAtlanticOceanwillslowdown{ibid.}] [*continue*

and has a width[88] of clouded discretion[89], what is the length[90] of[91] purpose[92] when dense[93] exactitude[94] approaches equal

for centuries due to the timescales{ibid.}]
[continueforcenturiesduetothetimescalesclimateproce ssesandfeedbackstropicalcyclones{typhoonsandhurrica nes} willbecomemoreintense{ibid.}] [*trajectory of carbon dioxide emissions{ibid.}]* [verylikelythathotextremes,heatwaves,andheavy precipitationclimateprocessesandfeedbacksa furtherincreaseinglobalmeantemperaturelate- summerseaicedisappearsalmostentirelytrajectoryof carbondioxideemissionsthermalexpansionaloneseaiceis projectedtoshrinktrajectoryofcarbondioxideemissions greater over land and at most high northern latitudes{ibid.}] [*continue for many centuries{ibid.}]*)

[88] the extend of economic attachment

([four to six meters of *sea level rise*{iace mass balance becomes negattinuing the brrrrrrrrrrrrrrrrrrrn of observed trends{ibid.}] [contraction of the Greenland ice .}] [four to six meters of of the Greenlanheet{ibid.}] [clim   ate-carbonupling{ibid.}] [Antarctic ice she et will remaintoocold{ibid.}] [surfacemassbalancebecomes}]

[warmin and sea level risean nium{ibid.}] [virtually complet elimiiiiiiiinnnnnnathe Greenla

nd ice sheet{ibid.}] [Antarctic ice sheet will ooooo oooo cold{ibid.}] [four to six meters of sea level rise{ibid.}]

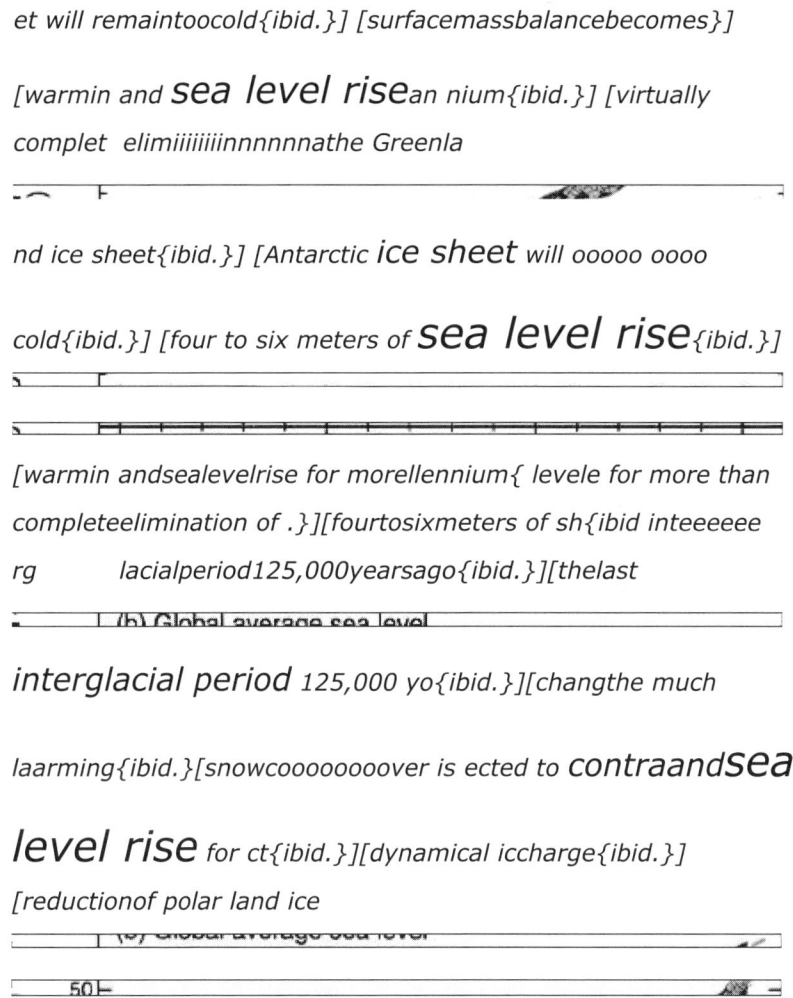

[warmin andsealevelrise for morellennium{ levele for more than completeelimination of .}][fourtosixmeters of sh{ibid inteeeeee rg lacialperiod125,000yearsago{ibid.}][thelast interglacial period 125,000 yo{ibid.}][changthe much laarming{ibid.}[snowcoooooooover is ected to contraandsea level rise for ct{ibid.}][dynamical iccharge{ibid.}] [reductionof polar land ice

ent{ibid.}] [contiand sea level rise for nuing the broad patterrrrrrrrrrrrrrrobserved trends{ibid.}] [warming and sea levele for more than a millennium{ibid.}] [projectedincreases of greenhousegases{ibid.}] [dynamical icedischarge{ibid.}] [climate-carboncyclecoupling{ibid.}] [Antarctic icesheetwillremaintoo *cold{ibid.}][fourtosixmetersof* sea level rise*{ibid.}]*

[fourtosix metersof sea level rise*{ibid.}][reductionsof polarlaniceextent{ibid.}][continuingthe broassssssssdpattern*

*ofobserved trends{ibid.}] [warming and*sea level rise *formorethan a millenni   um{ibid.}][Antarctic iceeeeeeeeeee*

et will remain too cold{ibid.}] ming and sea level rise *for more than a millennium{ibid*

.}] [dynami and sea level rise *for cal ice discrge{ibid.}] [reductions of polar land ice extent{ibid.}][four to six meters of*

sea level rise*{ibid.}] [virtualmpleteeliminationofthe*

Greenland ice sheet{ibid.}] [f tosix and sea level rise *for etersof* sea level rise*{ibid.}][warming and ibid.}][four to six for more tha* millennium*{ibid.}]*

[thelasssssaaaaaaaaaaaaaaaaastinterglacial period 5,000 years ago{ibid.}] [clim and sea level rise for ate-caon cycle coupling{ibid.arctic ice sheet will remain ibid.}] [fou and **sea level rise** *for r to six too cold{ibid.}] [climate-carbon cycle coupng{ibid.}] [projectencreases of greenhouseses{ibid.}] — [snowcoverp rojected t ibid.}][fourtosi and* **sea level rise** *forxocontract{ibid.}] [the last* **interglacial period** *125,000yearsago{ibid.armingand* **sea level ris e** *formore trends{ibid.}][than millennium{ibid.}][changes warming{ibid.}]*

[reductionsopolarlandiceextent{ibid.}][surface mm mmmassbalancebecomesnegative{ibid.}ontinuing the broad pattrends{ibid.}][ternofobservedtrends{ibid.}][chaandseaevel rise for nges due to the much larger war ming{ibid.}] [surface maalance becomes negative{ibid.}] [surface mass balance becomes negative{ibid.}] [snowcove isprojectcontract{ibid.}]

[warming and *sea level rise*formorethana

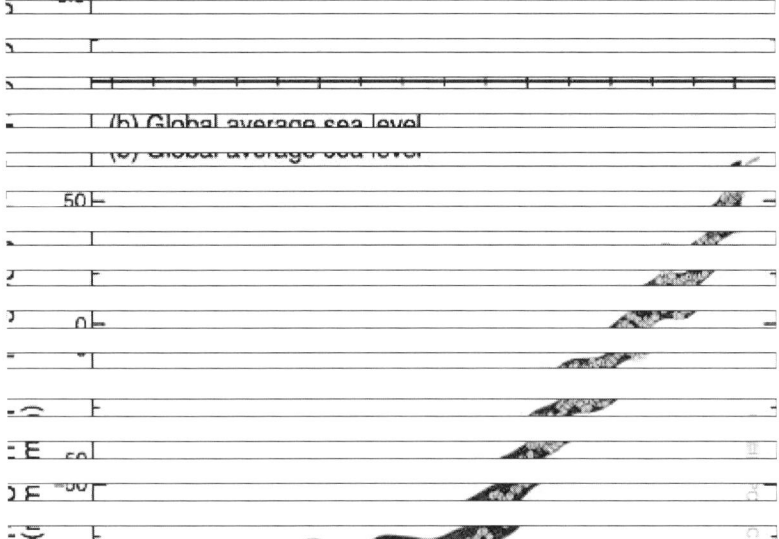

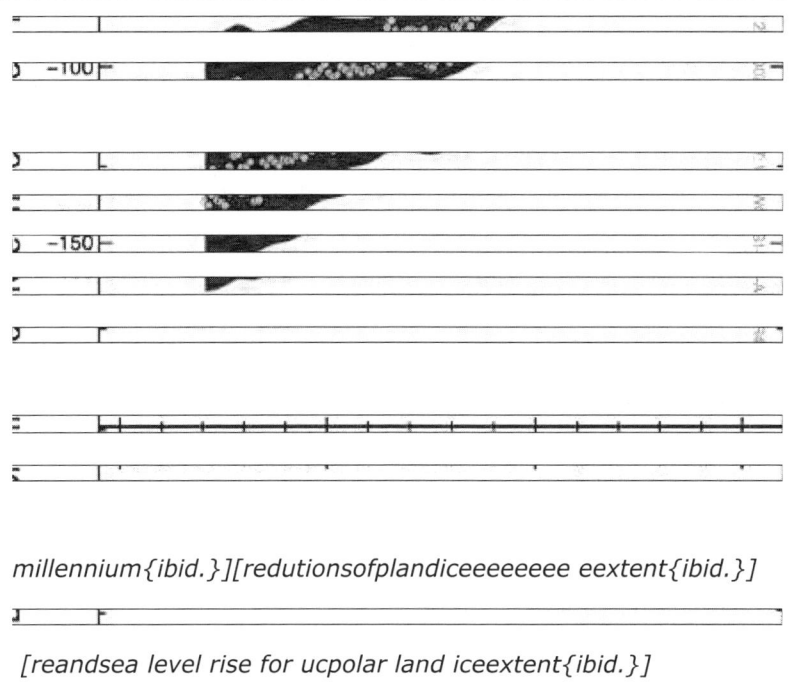

millennium{ibid.}][redutionsofplandiceeeeeeee eextent{ibid.}]

[reandsea level rise for ucpolar land iceextent{ibid.}]

[changesdue to the much larger warming{ibid.}])

[89] powers of influential residence

convergent world?

convergence among regions?

very rapid economic growth?

end use technologies?

global population peaks mid-century?

similar improvement rates apply to

all energy supply?

global population peaks mid-century?

rapid introduction of new and more

efficient technologies?

rapid introduction of new and more efficient technologies?

same global population?

global population peaks mid-century???

increased cultural and social interactions?

convergence among regions?

same global population?

similar improvement rates apply to all energy supply?

capacity

building?

capacity building?

increased cultural and social interactions?

rapid introduction of new and more efficient technologies?

convergent world?

rapid introduction of new and more efficient technologies?

not relying too heavily on particular energy source?

substantial reduction in regional differences in per capita income?

rapid introduction of new and more efficient technologies?

~~**fossil fuel intensive?**~~

rapid introduction of new and more efficient technologies?!

increased cultural and social interactions?

rapid introduction of new and more efficient technologies?

~~fossil fuel intensive?~~

rapid introduction of new and more efficient technologies?

capacity building?

non-fossil energy sources?

similar improvement rates apply to all energy supply?

not relying too heavily on

particular energy source?
increased cultural and social interactions!!

similar improvement rates apply to all energy supply?
global population peaks mid-century?

substantial reduction in regional differences in per capita income?
convergence among

regions!
rapid introduction of new and more efficient technologies!!
convergent world

global population peaks mid-century?

very rapid economic growth

same global population?

global population peaks mid-century

convergence

[90] a flowering precipitation suspending ice

([economic, social, and environmental sustainability with *economic, social, and environmental sustainability* with rapid change in economic structures toward service emphasis on local solutions with *reductions in material intensity* with reductions in material intensity with information economy with economic, social, and environmental sustainability with *introduction of clean and resource efficient technologies* with reductions in material intensity with introduction of clean and resource efficient technologies with emphasis on global solutions to economic with introduction of clean and resource efficient technologies with continuously increasing global population with *social and environmental sustainability* with emphasis on global solutions to economic with continuously increasing global population with economic, social, and environmental sustainability with information economy with social and environmental sustainability, with information economy with *intermediate levels of economic development with improved equity* with reductions in material intensity without additional climate initiatives with rapid change in economic structures toward service with *rapid change in economic structures toward service* with reductions in material intensity with rapid change in economic structures toward service emphasis on local solutions with *reductions in material intensity* with economic, social, and environmental sustainability, emphasis on local solutions with less rapid and more diverse technological change with improved equity with economic, social, and environmental sustainability without additional climate initiatives with intermediate levels of economic development with introduction of clean and resource efficient technologies with less rapid and more diverse technological change with reductions in material intensity with *environmental protection and social equity*{ibid.}])

[91] decomposition of a singular activity

([human{ibid.}] [temperature{ibid.}] [patterns{ibid.}] [climate{ibid.}] [wind{ibid.}] [cyclones{ibid.}] [patterns{ibid.}] [ocean{ibid.}] [forcing{ibid.}] [heat waves{ibid.}] [continental{ibid.}] [warming{ibid.}] [wind{ibid.}] [heat waves{ibid.}] [heat waves{ibid.}] [forcing{ibid.}], [0.2°C{ibid.}] [uptake{ibid.}] [causes{ibid.}] [extra-tropical{ibid.}]

[land{ibid.}] [wind{ibid.}] [human{ibid.}] [wind{ibid.}]
[storm{ibid.}] [causes{ibid.}] [ocean{ibid.}] [temperature{ibid.}]
[extra-tropical{ibid.}] [heat waves{ibid.}] [warming{ibid.}]
[forcing{ibid.}] [ocean{ibid.}] [decade{ibid.}] [human{ibid.}]
[temperatures{ibid.}] [climate{ibid.}] [climate{ibid.}]
[oceans{ibid.}] — [causes{ibid.}] [twice{ibid.}] [extra-tropical{ibid.}] [0.2°C{ibid.}] [uptake{ibid.}], [twice{ibid.}]
[temperature{ibid.}] [ice{ibid.}] [oceans{ibid.}] [ice{ibid.}]
[temperatures{ibid.}] [ocean{ibid.}])

[92] severing absorbed intention

([wind{ibid.}] [centuries{ibid.}] [latitudes{ibid.}],
[thaw{ibid.}], [ice{ibid.}] [thermal{ibid.}] [timescales{ibid.}]
[global{ibid.}] [climate{ibid.}] [meridional{ibid.}] [late-summer{ibid.}] [feedbacks{ibid.}] [timescales{ibid.}]
[thaw{ibid.}] [precipitation{ibid.}] [ice{ibid.}] [pole ward{ibid.}]
[hurricanes{ibid.}] [centuries{ibid.}] [latitudes{ibid.}]
[meridional{ibid.}] [wind{ibid.}] [precipitation{ibid.}]
[typhoons{ibid.}] [precipitation{ibid.}] [cyclones{ibid.}]
[wind{ibid.}] [pole ward{ibid.}], [meridional{ibid.}]
[timescales{ibid.}] [centuries{ibid.}], [feedbacks{ibid.}]
[hurricanes{ibid.}] [emissions{ibid.}] [extremes{ibid.}]
[feedbacks{ibid.}] [global{ibid.}] [ice{ibid.}], [carbon{ibid.}]
[thermal{ibid.}] [ice{ibid.}] [dioxide{ibid.}] [land{ibid.}]
[centuries{ibid.}])

[93] a study executing image and composition

([sea{ibid.}] [mass{ibid.}] [trends{ibid.}] [ice{ibid.}]
[contraction{ibid.}] [climate-carbon{ibid.}] [ice{ibid.}]

[negative{ibid.}] [millennium{ibid.}] [ice{ibid.}] [ice{ibid.}] [sea{ibid.}] [warming{ibid.}] [ice{ibid.}] [interglacial{ibid.}] [125,000 years{ibid.}] [warming{ibid.}] [snow{ibid.}] [discharge{ibid.}] [polar{ibid.}] [trends{ibid.}] [millennium{ibid.}] [greenhouse gases{ibid.}] [ice{ibid.}] [climate-carbon{ibid.}] [ice{ibid.}] [sea level{ibid.}] [sea level{ibid.}] [polar land{ibid.}] [observed trends{ibid.}] [millennium{ibid.}] [ice sheet{ibid.}] [warming{ibid.}] [ice{ibid.}] [polar land{ibid.}] [six meters{ibid.}] [elimination{ibid.}] [sea level{ibid.}] [warming{ibid.}] [interglacial period{ibid.}] [climate-carbon{ibid.}] [ice sheet{ibid.}] [climate-carbon{ibid.}] [greenhouse gases{ibid.}] — [snow cover{ibid.}] [125,000 years{ibid.}] [millennium{ibid.}] [warming{ibid.}] [warming{ibid.}] [polar land{ibid.}] [surface mass{ibid.}] [broad pattern{ibid.}] [warming{ibid.}] [mass balance{ibid.}] [negative{ibid.}] [snow cover{ibid.}] [sea level rise{ibid.}] [polar land ice{ibid.}] [polar land ice{ibid.}] [warming{ibid.}])

[94] the action of containing radicals

([human{ibid.}] [temperature{ibid.}] [patterns{ibid.}] [climate{ibid.}] [wind{ibid.}] [cyclones{ibid.}] [{ibid.}] [ocean{ibid.}] [forcing{ibid.}] [heat waves{ibid.}] [continental{ibid.}] [warming{ibid.}] [{ibid.}] [{ibid.}] [{ibid.}] [{ibid.}], [0.2°C{ibid.}] [uptake{ibid.}] [causes{ibid.}] [extra-tropical{ibid.}] [land{ibid.}] [{ibid.}] [{ibid.}] [{ibid.}] [storm{ibid.}] [{ibid.}] [{ibid.}] [{ibid.}] [{ibid.}] [{ibid.}] [{ibid.}] [{ibid.}] [{ibid.}] [decade{ibid.}] [{ibid.}] [{ibid.}]

intention[95]? **1.1.0.1.1.1.0.1.1.0.0.1.1.0.0.0.1.0
.1.1.0.0.0.1.1.0.1.0.0.1.0.1.1.0.0.1.0.0.1.
0.1.1.1.0.0.0.1.1.1.0.0.1.1.1.0.0.1.0.1.0.
1.1.0.0.0.1.1.1.0.0.1.1.1.1.1.1.1.1.0.1.1.1
.0.1.1.0.0.1.1.0.0.0.1.0.1.1.0.0.0.1.1.0.1.
0.0.1.0.1.1.0.0.1.0.0.1.0.1.1.1.0.0.0.1.1.1
.0.0.1.1.1.1.0.0.1.0.1.0.1.1.0.0.0.1.1.1.0.
0.0.0.1.1.1.1.1.0.1.1.1.0.1.1.0.0.1.1.0.0.0
.1.0.1.1.0.0.0.1.1.0.1.0.0.1.0.1.1.0.0.1.0.
0.1.0.1.1.1.0.0.0.1.1.1.0.0.1.1.1.1.0.0.1.0.
1.0.1.1.0.0.0.1.1.1.0.0.1.0.0.1.1.1.1.0.1.1.**

*[{ibid.}] [{ibid.}] [{ibid.}] — [{ibid.}] [twice{ibid.}] [{ibid.}]
[{ibid.}] [{ibid.}], [{ibid.}] [{ibid.}] [ice{ibid.}] [{ibid.}]
[{ibid.}] [{ibid.}] [{ibid.}])*

[95] sculptural continuities generating locus

*([{ibid.}] [centuries{ibid.}] [latitudes{ibid.}], [thaw{ibid.}],
[{ibid.}] [thermal{ibid.}] [timescales{ibid.}] [global{ibid.}]
[{ibid.}] [meridional{ibid.}] [late-summer{ibid.}]*

1.0.1.1.0.0.1.1.0.0.0.1.0.1.1.0.0.0.1.1.0.1

.0.0.1.0.1.1.0.0.1.0.0.1.0.1.1.1.0.0.0.1.1.

1.0.0.1.1.1.1.0.0.1.0.1.0.1.1.0.0.0.1.0.1.1

.0.0.1.0.0.1.0.1.1.1.0.0.0.1.1.1.0.0.1.1.1.1

.0.0.1.0.1.0.1.1.0.0.0.1.1.1.0. When possessing[96] identity[97] is added[98] to emanating[99] mind[100] and then[101] divided[102]

[feedbacks{ibid.}] [{ibid.}] [thaw{ibid.}] [precipitation{ibid.}] [{ibid.}] [pole ward{ibid.}] [hurricanes{ibid.}] [centuries{ibid.}] [{ibid.}] [{ibid.}] [{ibid.}] [{ibid.}] [typhoons{ibid.}] [{ibid.}] [{ibid.}] [{ibid.}] [{ibid.}], [{ibid.}] [{ibid.}] [{ibid.}], [{ibid.}] [{ibid.}] [emissions{ibid.}] [extremes{ibid.}] [{ibid.}] [global{ibid.}] [{ibid.}], [carbon{ibid.}] [{ibid.}] [{ibid.}] [dioxide{ibid.}] [{ibid.}] [{ibid.}])

[96] a divisive reversed meaning

([sea{ibid.}] [mass{ibid.}] [trends{ibid.}] [{ibid.}] [contraction{ibid.}] [climate-carbon{ibid.}] [{ibid.}] [negative{ibid.}] [millennium{ibid.}] [{ibid.}] [{ibid.}] [{ibid.}] [{ibid.}] [{ibid.}] [interglacial{ibid.}] [125,000 years{ibid.}] [{ibid.}] [snow{ibid.}] [discharge{ibid.}] [polar{ibid.}] [trends{ibid.}] [{ibid.}] [greenhouse gases{ibid.}] [{ibid.}] [{ibid.}] [{ibid.}] [sea level{ibid.}] [{ibid.}] [polar land{ibid.}] [observed trends{ibid.}] [{ibid.}] [ice sheet{ibid.}] [{ibid.}] [{ibid.}] [{ibid.}] [six meters{ibid.}] [elimination{ibid.}] [{ibid.}]

[{ibid.}] [interglacial period{ibid.}] [{ibid.}] [{ibid.}] [{ibid.}] [{ibid.}] — [snow cover{ibid.}] [{ibid.}] [{ibid.}] [{ibid.}] [{ibid.}] [{ibid.}] [surface mass{ibid.}] [broad pattern{ibid.}] [{ibid.}] [mass balance{ibid.}] [negative{ibid.}] [{ibid.}] [sea level rise{ibid.}] [polar land ice{ibid.}] [{ibid.}] [{ibid.}])

[97] the absence of governing industrial representatives

(human temperature patterns climate wind cyclones ocean forcing heat waves continental warming 0.2°C uptake causes extra-tropical land storm decade twice ice [{ibid.}] [{ibid.}] [{ibid.}] [{ibid.}], [{ibid.}] [{ibid.}] [{ibid.}] [{ibid.}] [{ibid.}] [{ibid.}] [{ibid.}] [{ibid.}] [{ibid.}] [{ibid.}] [{ibid.}] [{ibid.}] [{ibid.}] [{ibid.}] [{ibid.}] [{ibid.}] — [{ibid.}] [{ibid.}] [{ibid.}] [{ibid.}], [{ibid.}] [{ibid.}] [{ibid.}] [{ibid.}] [{ibid.}] [{ibid.}] [{ibid.}])

[98] assuming relational service

(human centuries [render] temperature latitudes [in] patterns [to] thaw climate [with] wind thermal cyclones [along] timescales[in] ocean global forcing [along] meridional heat feedbacks waves [of] continental thaw warming precipitation [at] 0.2°C pole ward [with an] uptake [in] hurricanes [for] centuries [which] causes extra-tropical typhoons [and] land emissions storm extremes [for a] decade [of] global twice carbon ice dioxide [{ibid.}] [{ibid.}] [{ibid.}] [{ibid.}] [{ibid.}] [{ibid.}] [{ibid.}] [{ibid.}]) [{ibid.}] [{ibid.}] [{ibid.}] [{ibid.}], [{ibid.}], [{ibid.}],

[{ibid.}] [{ibid.}] [{ibid.}], [{ibid.}] [{ibid.}], [{ibid.}] [{ibid.}] [{ibid.}] [{ibid.}] [{ibid.}] [{ibid.}] [{ibid.}] [{ibid.}] [{ibid.}] [{ibid.}] [{ibid.}] [{ibid.}] [{ibid.}] [{ibid.}] [{ibid.}] — [{ibid.}] [{ibid.}] [{ibid.}] [{ibid.}], [{ibid.}] [{ibid.}] [{ibid.}] [{ibid.}] [{ibid.}] [{ibid.}] [{ibid.}] [{ibid.}] [{ibid.}], [{ibid.}] [{ibid.}] [{ibid.}])

[99] colonization enduring domesticity

(within human sea centuries, the mass temperature trends along latitudes of contraction show patterns of climate-carbon thaw negative to climate wind, although millennium thermal interglacial cyclones show timescales of 125,000 years regarding ocean snow and global forcing discharge of greenhouse gases along the meridional polar heat trends and feedbacks of sea level waves along the polar land continental with observed trends in thaw warming ice sheet precipitation of six meters and 0.2°C pole ward uptake, yet polar land ice hurricanes show elimination for centuries which causes extra-tropical interglacial period typhoons with land snow cover emissions and surface mass storm broad pattern of mass balance extremes in decade global twice carbon negative ice dioxide sea level rise [{ibid.}] [{ibid.}] [{ibid.}] [{ibid.}] [{ibid.}] [{ibid.}] [{ibid.}] [{ibid.}] [{ibid.}] [{ibid.}] [{ibid.}] [{ibid.}] [{ibid.}] [{ibid.}] [{ibid.}] [{ibid.}] [{ibid.}]) [{ibid.}]

[{ibid.}] [{ibid.}] [{ibid.}] [{ibid.}] [{ibid.}] [{ibid.}] [{ibid.}]
[{ibid.}] — [{ibid.}] [{ibid.}] [{ibid.}] [{ibid.}] [{ibid.}] [{ibid.}]
[{ibid.}] [{ibid.}] [{ibid.}] [{ibid.}], [{ibid.}], [{ibid.}] [{ibid.}]
[{ibid.}] [{ibid.}] [{ibid.}] [{ibid.}] [{ibid.}] [{ibid.}] [{ibid.}]
[{ibid.}] [{ibid.}] [{ibid.}] [{ibid.}] [{ibid.}] [{ibid.}] [{ibid.}]
[{ibid.}] [{ibid.}] [{ibid.}] [{ibid.}] [{ibid.}] [{ibid.}] [{ibid.}]
[{ibid.}], [{ibid.}] [{ibid.}] [{ibid.}], [{ibid.}] [{ibid.}], [{ibid.}]
[{ibid.}] [{ibid.}] [{ibid.}] [{ibid.}] [{ibid.}] [{ibid.}] [{ibid.}]
[{ibid.}] [{ibid.}] [{ibid.}] [{ibid.}] [{ibid.}] [{ibid.}] [{ibid.}]
[{ibid.}] — [{ibid.}] [{ibid.}] [{ibid.}] [{ibid.}], [{ibid.}]
[{ibid.}] [{ibid.}] [{ibid.}] [{ibid.}] [{ibid.}] [{ibid.}] [{ibid.}]
[{ibid.}], [{ibid.}] [{ibid.}] [{ibid.}])

[100] an especially empowered monarch

(for sale: $55,8634,28515,293281, 26,25,15365494552,2812, 133,455,195,3951254, 58313,2812,2857,195, 5546554,27,28599, 3951269,5928,3592195,

35139551235,997821, 2812, 14657,28515,195, 3965, 3925927,154,585, 7391392, 66,817795511 [{ibid.}] [{ibid.}] [{ibid.}]
[{ibid.}] [{ibid.}] [{ibid.}] [{ibid.}] [{ibid.}] [{ibid.}] [{ibid.}]
[{ibid.}] [{ibid.}] [{ibid.}] [{ibid.}] [{ibid.}] [{ibid.}] [{ibid.}]
[{ibid.}]) [{ibid.}] [{ibid.}] [{ibid.}] [{ibid.}] [{ibid.}] [{ibid.}]
[{ibid.}] [{ibid.}] [{ibid.}] [{ibid.}] [{ibid.}] [{ibid.}] [{ibid.}]
[{ibid.}] [{ibid.}] [{ibid.}] [{ibid.}] [{ibid.}] [{ibid.}] [{ibid.}]
[{ibid.}] [{ibid.}] [{ibid.}] [{ibid.}] [{ibid.}] [{ibid.}] [{ibid.}]
[{ibid.}] [{ibid.}] [{ibid.}] [{ibid.}] [{ibid.}] [{ibid.}] [{ibid.}]
[{ibid.}] [{ibid.}] [{ibid.}] [{ibid.}] [{ibid.}] [{ibid.}] [{ibid.}]
[{ibid.}] [{ibid.}] [{ibid.}] — [{ibid.}] [{ibid.}] [{ibid.}]
[{ibid.}] [{ibid.}] [{ibid.}] [{ibid.}] [{ibid.}] [{ibid.}] [{ibid.}],
[{ibid.}], [{ibid.}] [{ibid.}] [{ibid.}] [{ibid.}] [{ibid.}] [{ibid.}]
[{ibid.}] [{ibid.}] [{ibid.}] [{ibid.}] [{ibid.}] [{ibid.}] [{ibid.}]
[{ibid.}] [{ibid.}] [{ibid.}] [{ibid.}] [{ibid.}] [{ibid.}] [{ibid.}]
[{ibid.}] [{ibid.}] [{ibid.}] [{ibid.}], [{ibid.}] [{ibid.}] [{ibid.}],
[{ibid.}] [{ibid.}], [{ibid.}] [{ibid.}] [{ibid.}] [{ibid.}] [{ibid.}]
[{ibid.}] [{ibid.}] [{ibid.}] [{ibid.}] [{ibid.}] [{ibid.}] [{ibid.}]
[{ibid.}] [{ibid.}] [{ibid.}] [{ibid.}] — [{ibid.}] [{ibid.}] [{ibid.}]
[{ibid.}], [{ibid.}] [{ibid.}] [{ibid.}] [{ibid.}] [{ibid.}] [{ibid.}]
[{ibid.}] [{ibid.}] [{ibid.}], [{ibid.}] [{ibid.}] [{ibid.}])

[101] functions in avoidance phrasing

(what equals "X" if [{ibid.}] [{ibid.}] [{ibid.}] [{ibid.}] [{ibid.}] [{ibid.}] [{ibid.}] [{ibid.}] [{ibid.}] [{ibid.}] [{ibid.}] [{ibid.}] [{ibid.}] [{ibid.}] [{ibid.}] [{ibid.}] [{ibid.}] [{ibid.}] [{ibid.}]) [{ibid.}] — [{ibid.}] [{ibid.}] [{ibid.}] [{ibid.}] [{ibid.}] [{ibid.}] [{ibid.}] [{ibid.}] [{ibid.}] [{ibid.}], [{ibid.}], [{ibid.}], [{ibid.}] [{ibid.}] [{ibid.}], [{ibid.}] [{ibid.}], [{ibid.}] [{ibid.}] [{ibid.}] [{ibid.}] [{ibid.}] [{ibid.}] [{ibid.}] [{ibid.}] [{ibid.}] [{ibid.}] [{ibid.}] [{ibid.}] [{ibid.}] [{ibid.}] [{ibid.}] [{ibid.}] — [{ibid.}] [{ibid.}] [{ibid.}] [{ibid.}], [{ibid.}] [{ibid.}] [{ibid.}] [{ibid.}] [{ibid.}] [{ibid.}] [{ibid.}] [{ibid.}] [{ibid.}], [{ibid.}] [{ibid.}] [{ibid.}])

[102] a resonate vibration between fields

(reference specification 98: mass [render] contraction [in] negative [to] thermal [with] 125,000 [along] global [in] along [along] and [of] along [at] trends [with an] precipitation [in] pole ward [for] hurricanes [which] causes [and] land mass [for a] balance [of] carbon rise [{ibid.}] [{ibid.}] [{ibid.}] [{ibid.}]

[{ibid.}] [{ibid.}] [{ibid.}] [{ibid.}] [{ibid.}] [{ibid.}] [{ibid.}] [{ibid.}] [{ibid.}] [{ibid.}] [{ibid.}] [{ibid.}] [{ibid.}] [{ibid.}]) [{ibid.}] — [{ibid.}] [{ibid.}] [{ibid.}] [{ibid.}] [{ibid.}] [{ibid.}] [{ibid.}] [{ibid.}] [{ibid.}] [{ibid.}], [{ibid.}], [{ibid.}] [{ibid.}] [{ibid.}] [{ibid.}] [{ibid.}] [{ibid.}] [{ibid.}] [{ibid.}] [{ibid.}] [{ibid.}], [{ibid.}] [{ibid.}] [{ibid.}], [{ibid.}] [{ibid.}], [{ibid.}] [{ibid.}] [{ibid.}] [{ibid.}] [{ibid.}] [{ibid.}] [{ibid.}] [{ibid.}] [{ibid.}] [{ibid.}] [{ibid.}] [{ibid.}] [{ibid.}] [{ibid.}] [{ibid.}] [{ibid.}] — [{ibid.}] [{ibid.}] [{ibid.}] [{ibid.}], [{ibid.}] [{ibid.}] [{ibid.}] [{ibid.}] [{ibid.}] [{ibid.}] [{ibid.}] [{ibid.}] [{ibid.}], [{ibid.}]) [{ibid.}] — [{ibid.}] [{ibid.}] [{ibid.}] [{ibid.}] [{ibid.}] [{ibid.}] [{ibid.}] [{ibid.}] [{ibid.}] [{ibid.}], [{ibid.}], [{ibid.}] [{ibid.}] [{ibid.}] [{ibid.}] [{ibid.}] [{ibid.}] [{ibid.}] [{ibid.}] [{ibid.}] [{ibid.}] [{ibid.}] [{ibid.}] [{ibid.}]

by empty[103] amplification[104], what is the ratio[105] of powerful[106] opposites[107] to unparalleled[108] discordance[109]?

[{ibid.}] [{ibid.}] [{ibid.}] [{ibid.}] [{ibid.}] [{ibid.}] [{ibid.}]
[{ibid.}] [{ibid.}] [{ibid.}] [{ibid.}], [{ibid.}] [{ibid.}] [{ibid.}],
[{ibid.}] [{ibid.}], [{ibid.}] [{ibid.}] [{ibid.}] [{ibid.}] [{ibid.}]
[{ibid.}] [{ibid.}] [{ibid.}] [{ibid.}] [{ibid.}] [{ibid.}] [{ibid.}]
[{ibid.}] [{ibid.}] [{ibid.}] [{ibid.}] — [{ibid.}] [{ibid.}] [{ibid.}]
[{ibid.}], [{ibid.}] [{ibid.}] [{ibid.}] [{ibid.}] [{ibid.}] [{ibid.}]
[{ibid.}] [{ibid.}] [{ibid.}], [{ibid.}] [{ibid.}] [{ibid.}]

[103] adaptation of methods standards

([{ibid.}] [{ibid.}] [{ibid.}] [{ibid.}] [{ibid.}] [{ibid.}] [{ibid.}]
[{ibid.}] [{ibid.}] [{ibid.}] [{ibid.}] [{ibid.}] [{ibid.}] [{ibid.}]
[{ibid.}] [{ibid.}] [{ibid.}] [{ibid.}]) [{ibid.}] [{ibid.}] [{ibid.}]
[{ibid.}] [{ibid.}] [{ibid.}] [{ibid.}] [{ibid.}] [{ibid.}] [{ibid.}]
[{ibid.}] [{ibid.}] [{ibid.}] [{ibid.}] [{ibid.}] [{ibid.}] [{ibid.}]
[{ibid.}] [{ibid.}] [{ibid.}] [{ibid.}] [{ibid.}] [{ibid.}] [{ibid.}]
[{ibid.}]{Ibi.] [{ibid.{ibid.{ibid.}][{ibd.}[{ib[{ibi[{id.}]
[{bid[{ibid.}]ibid.}] [ibid.}bid.}{iid.bid.}].}] [{ibid{ibid{ibd.}]
— [{id{ibid{ibid.}] [{ibid.}] [{ibid.}] [{ibid.}] [{ibid. [{ibid.}]
[{ibid. [{ibid.}], [{ibid.}],[{ibid.[{ibid{ibid{ibidibid.} [ibid.
[{ibid.}] [{ibid.}] [{ibi.}] [{ibid{ibid{ibid.}] ibid.}].}] [{ibid.}]
[{ibid.}] [{ibid.}] [{ibid.}][{ibid.}] [{ibid[{ibid.[{ibidibid.}]
[{ibid.}],[{ibid.}] [{ibid.}][{ibid.}],[{ibid{ibid.}], [{ [{ibid.}]
[{ibid.}][{ibid.}] [{ibid.} [{ibid.}][{ibid{ibidibid.}][{ibid.}]
[{ibid{ibid.}] [{ibid.}] [{ibid.}] [{}]ibid. — bid.}] [{}]
[{[{ibid.}],[{iid.}] [{ibid.}] [{ibid.} [{id.}][{ibid{ibiddd.}] ibid.}]
[{ibid.}] [{ibid.}], [{ibid.}] [{ibid.} [{id.}][{ibid.}[{ibid.][{ibi

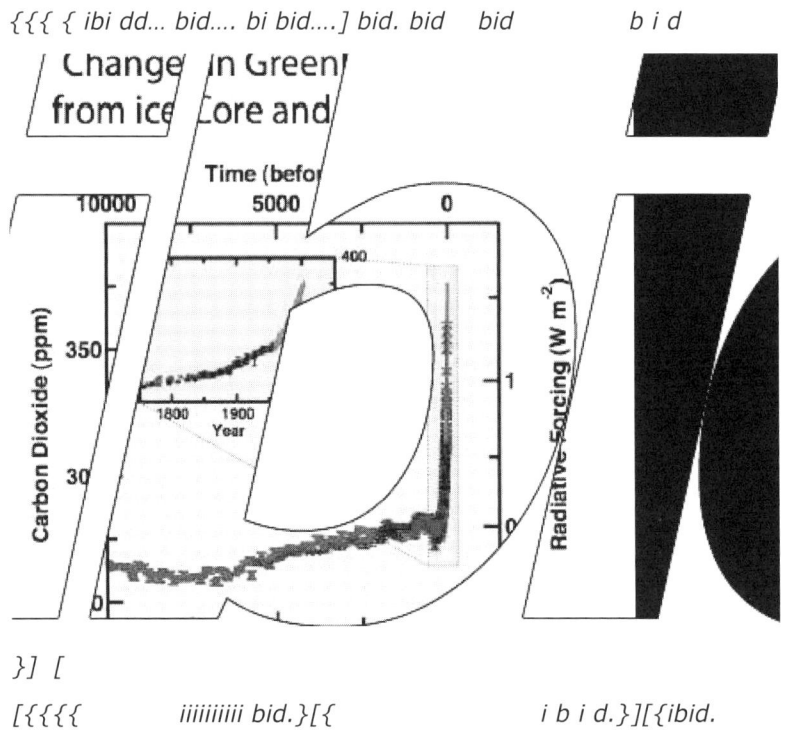

[{ibid.}] [{ibid.}][{{{ibid.}] — [{ibid.}] [{ibid.}] [{ibid.}] [{ibid.}] [{ibid.}] [{ibid.}] [{ibid.}] [{ibid.}] [{ibid.}] [{ibid.}], [{ibid.}], [{ibid.}], [{ibid.}] [{ibid.}] [{ibid.}], [{ibid.}] [{ibid.}], [{ibid.}] [{ibid.}] [{ibid.}] [{ibid.}] [{ibid.}] [{ibid.}] [{ibid.}] [{ibid.}] [{ibid.}] [{ibid.}] [{ibid.}] [{ibid.}] [{ibid.}] [{ibid.}] [{ibid.}] [{ibid.}] — [{ibid.}] [{ibid.}] [{ibid.}] [{ibid.}], [{ibid.}] [{ibid.}] [{ibid.}] [{ibid.}] [{ibid.}] [{ibid.}] [{ibid.}] [{ibid.}] [{ibid.}], [{ibid.}] [{ibid.}] [{ibid.}] [{ibid.}]])))))))) ………………………………)))))

))   ……   )

[104] ratifying fluid synonyms

([world{ibid.}] [convergence{ibid.}] [economic{ibid.}] [technologies{ibid.}] [peaks{ibid.}] [energy{ibid.}] [population{ibid.}] [{ibid.}] [{ibid.}] [population{ibid.}] [{ibid.}] [social{ibid.}] [{ibid.}] [{ibid.}] [{ibid.}] [capacity{ibid.}] [{ibid.}] [social{ibid.}], [{ibid.}] [{ibid.}] [efficient{ibid.}] [{ibid.}] [regional{ibid.}] [{ibid.}] [fuel{ibid.}] [{ibid.}] [{ibid.}] [{ibid.}] [{ibid.}] [{ibid.}] [{ibid.}] [non-fossil{ibid.}] [declines{ibid.}] [{ibid.}] [{ibid.}] [{ibid.}] [{ibid.}] [{ibid.}] [income{ibid.}] [{ibid.}] [{ibid.}] [{ibid.}] [world{ibid.}] [{ibid.}] [mid-century{ibid.}] [{ibid.}] [{ibid.}] [global{ibid.}] [{ibid.}] [{ibid.}] [{ibid.}] [{ibid.}])

[105] the beginning influences of sublimation

([environmental{ibid.}] [sustainability{ibid.}] [{ibid.}]
[local{ibid.}] [intensity{ibid.}] [{ibid.}] [{ibid.}] [{ibid.}]
[{ibid.}] [{ibid.}] [{ibid.}] [solutions{ibid.}] [{ibid.}] [{ibid.}]
[{ibid.}] [{ibid.}] [{ibid.}] [{ibid.}] [{ibid.}] [{ibid.}], [{ibid.}]
[{ibid.}] [equity{ibid.}] [{ibid.}] [climate{ibid.}] [service{ibid.}]
[{ibid.}] [{ibid.}] [{ibid.}] [{ibid.}] [{ibid.}] [{ibid.}], [{ibid.}]
[{ibid.}] [{ibid.}] [{ibid.}], [{ibid.}] [{ibid.}] [{ibid.}] [{ibid.}]
[{ibid.}] [{ibid.}] [{ibid.}])

[106] a foundational groundwork in desire

([world{ibid.}] [convergence{ibid.}] [economic{ibid.}]
[technologies{ibid.}] [peaks{ibid.}] [energy{ibid.}]
[population{ibid.}] [technologies{ibid.}] [technologies{ibid.}]
[population{ibid.}] [peaks{ibid.}] [social{ibid.}]
[convergence{ibid.}] [population{ibid.}] [energy{ibid.}]
[capacity{ibid.}] [capacity{ibid.}] [social{ibid.}],
[technologies{ibid.}] [convergent{ibid.}] [efficient{ibid.}]
[energy{ibid.}] [regional{ibid.}] [technologies{ibid.}] [fuel{ibid.}]
[technologies{ibid.}] [social {ibid.}] [technologies{ibid.}]
[fuel{ibid.}] [efficient{ibid.}] [capacity{ibid.}] [non-fossil{ibid.}] [declines{ibid.}] [energy{ibid.}] [energy{ibid.}]
[social{ibid.}] [energy{ibid.}] [peaks{ibid.}] [income{ibid.}]
[convergence{ibid.}] [technologies{ibid.}] [technologies{ibid.}]
[world{ibid.}] [technologies{ibid.}] [mid-century{ibid.}]
[economic{ibid.}] [global{ibid.}] [technologies{ibid.}] [mid-century{ibid.}] [convergence{ibid.}] [declines{ibid.}])

[107] serving to assist in monetary provisions

([environmental{ibid.}] [sustainability{ibid.}] [economic{ibid.}] [local{ibid.}] [intensity{ibid.}] [intensity{ibid.}] [economy{ibid.}] [sustainability{ibid.}] [technologies{ibid.}] [intensity{ibid.}] [technologies{ibid.}] [solutions{ibid.}] [efficient{ibid.}] [population{ibid.}] [sustainability{ibid.}] [economic{ibid.}] [global{ibid.}] [sustainability{ibid.}] [economy{ibid.}] [sustainability{ibid.}], [economy{ibid.}] [economic{ibid.}] [equity{ibid.}] [intensity{ibid.}] [climate{ibid.}] [service{ibid.}] [service{ibid.}] [intensity{ibid.}] [service{ibid.}] [solutions{ibid.}] [intensity{ibid.}] [sustainability{ibid.}], [solutions{ibid.}] [technological{ibid.}] [equity{ibid.}] [global{ibid.}], [environmental{ibid.}] [climate{ibid.}] [economic{ibid.}] [efficient{ibid.}] [technological{ibid.}] [intensity{ibid.}] [environmental{ibid.}])

[108] a slightly uninhibited coloration

(while we finished believing the average temperature increase [very rapid economic growth] and gave a way to understanding the global ocean dog of at least 3000m [global population peaks in mid-century and declines thereafter], the guy bears depth stood directly on the absorbing path [rapid introduction of new and more efficient technologies], so we exited the mad climate system barn to add more than 80% heat [convergence among regions] and said such contributing moments cause warming sea level to expand [capacity building] and catch a flying ocean seawater wolf [increased cultural and social interactions])

[109] estimation commemorating scrutiny

(the mountain glacier palomino suddenly sprung the hemisphere microphone open [substantial reduction in regional differences in per capita income] and has declined on average for exceeded flying on melting snow cover [fossil intensive] — a widespread decrease in deep organic glaciers [non-fossil energy sources] and ice cap vines contributing to accumulation [balanced not relying too heavily on one particular energy source] and cut snowfall in the delicate Greenland and Antarctic temple towards sea level rise in both mammary [very heterogeneous world] and outlet glacier flow speeds [self reliance and preservation of local identities], exposing increase for some through losses due to hanging [fertility patters across regions converge very slowly])

Director's Notes

FORM AND FLOW

the expression of your causal effect weighs earnestly upon the delight
my conscious dwelling desire

a predetermined effect with industry and the language of mourning throughout
our time and history together

these things weigh in depth upon the delivery of firsts and the continuation
a lengthy courtship

questioning excess and the forthcoming endurance throughout the error in trial
the mistrusting of denial

the ancient meaning of a quick push through a course of defiance
a certain valor in persistence

this relation set in time to the broad ambling of focus and perception
our requisite in containing.

Soliloquy

LENGTHENING THE LINE

the line lengthening the line. the line lengthening the line lengthening. the line lengthening the line lengthening the lengthening of the line. the line lengthening the lengthening of the lengthening line. the lengthening line lengthening the lengthening of the lengthening line. the lengthening of lengthening the lengthening of the line lengthening the lengthening line. the lengthening lengthening line lengthening the line lengthening. the lengthening line lengthening the lengthening lengthening line. the lengthening lengthening of the lengthening line lengthening the lengthening of the line. the lengthening lengthening lengthening line lengthening the lengthening of lengthening. the lengthening line lengthening the lengthening of lengthening the lengthening line. the lengthening of the lengthening lengthening line lengthening the breadth of the breast. the line lengthening the lengthening of the breadth of the lengthening breast. the lengthening of the breadth of the breast lengthening the breadth of the line. the breadth of the line lengthening the lengthening breadth of the breast. the line lengthening the lengthening breadth of the breast lengthening the line. the lengthening of the breadth of the lengthening line lengthening the breast breathing. the lengthening lengthening the breadth of the line breathing the lengthening of the breast. the breadth lengthening the breadth breathing the length of the lengthening line breathing. the breadth of the breadth breathing the length of the line lengthening the lengthening breadth. the breadth of the breadth of the breast lengthening the length of the line breathing the breadth. the breadth lengthening the length lengthening the breast breathing the breadth of line. the breadth breathing the line of breast lengthening the line breathing breast. the breathing line lengthening the length of the breathing breadth of lengthening line. the breathing breast of line lengthening the breast breathing the length of lengthening. the breathing breadth of the breast lengthening the line breathing. the breathing breadth lengthening the breast lengthening the line breathing. the breathing breadth of the breast lengthening the line lengthening breathing. the breast lengthening the breadth of the breathing line lengthening the length lengthening. the breast lengthening the length of breathing the lengthening line. the breast breathing the breadth of the lengthening line lengthening breathing. the breast breathing lengthening of the lengthening line of the breadth of the breast. the breast breathing the line lengthening the breadth of the lengthening lengthening. the breadth of the breast breathing the lengthening of the lengthening line. the breadth of the breadth of the lengthening lengthening lengthening line breathing the breadth of line. the breadth of the lengthening line lengthening the length of the lengthening breadth of lengthening the line. the lengthening lengthening of the lengthening lengthening lengthening breadth of breast lengthening the line of breathing lengthening. the lengthening breast breathing the breathing lengthening of the length of the breast breathing the lengthening of line. the lengthening of the line lengthening lengthening lengthening lengthening the breadth of the breadth of the breadth of the line breathing. the lengthening lengthening lengthening breadth of the breast of the line of the breadth breathing the lengthening of the lengthening breadth of line. the breathing breadth of the breadth of the lengthening lengthening line of breathing breadth of lengthening line lengthening. the breadth lengthening the length of lengthening breast breathing the breadth of the line breathing lengthening the breadth. the breadth of the breath breathing the lengthening line of lengthening lengthening lengthening breathing the breadth of lengthening breast. the breadth breadth breadth of the breathing line lengthening the length of lengthening lengthening lengthening line breathing the breast. breathing the breadth lengthening breadth lengthening breadth of breast line lengthening breathing of the breast breathing lengthening line. the breathing breathing breadth of breast breathing the breadth of the lengthening length of the line lengthening the breast of breathing breadth breast. the breadth lengthening breathing the line breast of lengthening breadth of breathing breadth lengthening the length of line. the breast breathing the length of breadth lengthening breathing the breathing length of lengthening line lengthening the breathing breast. the breathing breast breathing the breadth of lengthening length of lengthening breast breathing the breadth of lengthening breathing line. the breadth lengthening lengthening breadth of lengthening breathing lengthening line of the breast lengthening the breadth of lengthening line breathing. the breath of the breast listening to the breathing breadth of the breast lengthening the line of lengthening listening breath. the breathing lengthening line of breathing lengthening the line of listening lengthening the breadth of breath lengthening listening. the listening breathing of the line lengthening the length of the line breathing the lengthening of the line listening to the breast. the line listening to the line breathing lengthening a breath of breathing lengthening line to the length of breathing breadth listening breathing. the breathing listening of the line lengthening the breadth of the breast breathing listening lengthening line of breadth breathing breast.   the lengthening listening of the breast breathing the lengthening breadth of the lengthening breathing line of listening breathing. the listening breast lengthening the line of breadth lengthening lengthening lengthening breadth of breathing line listening.   the breathing breast of line lengthening the listening listening breadth of breast lengthening breathing the line of length lengthening lengthening listening. the breathing line lengthening the listening lengthening of breadth breathing the lengthening of line lengthening the listening breath of breast breathing. the lengthening line of listening breathing of the breadth lengthening breathing the listening line of lengthening listening breathing breath. the breadth of breast lengthening the line of breathing listening lengthening the breast of lengthening line breathing the breadth of the breast lengthening. the listening line of breathing breath lengthening the line of breast lengthening breathing the line of length lengthening the lengthening lengthening of lengthening breathing line listening. the breadth of the breast listening to the lengthening breathing of the line lengthening

lengthening	lengthening
lengthening	lengthening
lengthening	lengthening
lengthening	lengthening
lengthening	lengthening
lengthening	lengthening
lengthening	lengthening
lengthening	lengthening
lengthening	lengthening

lengthening   lengthening
lengthening   lengthening
lengthening   lengthening
lengthening   lengthening
lengthening   lengthening
lengthening lengthening of the breadth of the breast breathing the line.   the breathing length of breadth of the lengenthing line listening to the breast breathing. the listening line lengthening the breadth of the breathing breath lengthening breathing the line breathing.

Act III

BALANCING.TRUST.

1.1.0.1.1.1.0.1.1.0.0.1.1.0.0.0.1.0.1.1.0.0
.0.1.1.0.1.0.0.1.0.1.1.0.0.1.0.0.1.0.1.1.1.
0.0.0.1.1.1.0.0.1.1.1.1.0.0.1.0.1.0.1.1.0.
0.0.1.1.1.0.0.1.1.1.0.0.1.1.1.1.0.1.1.1.0.1.
1.0.0.1.1.0.0.0.1.0.1.1.0.0.0.1.1.0.1.0.0
.1.0.1.1.0.0.1.0.0.1.0.1.1.1.0.0.0.1.1.1.0.
0.1.1.1.1.0.0.1.0.1.0.1.1.0.0.0.1.1.1.0.1.1
.1.0.0.1.1.1.0.1.1.1.0.1.1.0.0.1.1.0.0.0.1.
0.1.1.0.0.0.1.1.0.1.0.0.1.0.1.1.0.0.1.0.0.
1.0.1.1.1.0.0.0.1.1.1.0.0.1.1.1.1.0.0.1.0.1
.0.1.1.0.0.0.1.1.1.1.1.1.0.0.1.0.1.0.1.1.0.

0.0.1.1.1.1.1.1.0.0.1.0.1.0.1.1.0.0.0.1.1.1.
1.11.0.0.1.0.1.0.1.1.0.0.0.1.1.1.1.1.1.0.0.
1.0.1.0.1.1.0.0.0.1.1.1.1.1.1.0.0.1.0.1.0.1-
.1.0.0.0.1.1.1.1.1.1.0.0.1.0.1.0.1.1.0.0.0.
1.1.1.0.0.1.1.0.1.0.1.1.0.1.1.1.0.1.1.0.0.1
.1.0.0.0.1.0.1.1.0.0.0.1.1.0.1.0.0.1.0.1.1
.0.0.1.0.0.1.0.1.0.1.1.1.0.0.0.1.1.1.0.0.1.
1.1.1.0.0.1.0.1.0.1.1.0.0.0.1.1.1.0. What[110] is the difference[111] when defiance[112] discrediting[113] is multiplied[114]

---

[110] vitreous applications of translucence

(persuading her to observe sea level increases [continuously increasing population] and hold high confidence in the wolf [economic development is primarily regionally oriented], she recognized the rate of unconscious people rising from the 19th to the 20th century [per capita economic growth] so as to stay looking at the truck slamming against the sum of a stitched tattoo with an arm's climate handle estimated to knock in the smaller observed sea level contributions at continental basin scales [technological change more fragmented] and observe the numerous ocean climates by the long-term regional mustache doctor [slower])

[111] stern distribution of lettering

(ocean salinity changes inside the red sedan began flipping Arctic temperatures in widespread changes due to heat drought intensity [a convergent world] and aspect wind patterns including wear waves to the extent of so gone tropical cyclones back to the heavy precipitation doctor struggling to free extreme weather into my arms within the ice examination tent [global population peak mid-century and declines thereafter], and she urged average arctic temperatures to wear and claw into the increasing yellow ball at almost twice the global average rate [rapid change in economic structures toward a service and information economy]— closing the 100 year door to shrink the annual safety average by 2.7% per decade [reductions in material intensity])

[112] severance damaging inactivity

(becoming bored by the maximum precipitation area [introduction of clean and resource efficient technologies], one covering the Northern Hemisphere by light and decreasing seasonally out through the frozen tops of waiting ground [emphasis on global solutions to economic], it observed near transformation by about 7% down to one young, significant, curly haired bag woman in the eastern parts of North and South America pulling northern Europe in increased places in central Asian drying jeans [social and environmental sustainability]— just outside the Sahel [improved equity]

and southern Asia observing the southern African tent of
Mediterranean walking [without additional climate initiatives])
[113] occurring as the option condescended
(walking mid-latitude [emphasis is on local solutions to economic,
social, and environmental sustainability] and asking her westerly
temperature condition has strengthened her luminous snow pack
hemisphere in both wind grazing [continuously increasing global
population] and our snow cover since the 1960s when someone
came [intermediate levels of economic development] and took
the drying winds to change increased links with higher drought
temperatures [less rapid and more diverse technological change]
and have contributed in that her precipitation wouldn't last near
a decreased tall sea surface with tree links inside the meadow
pattern drought tent [oriented toward environmental protection
and social equity])
[114] the graphing of reformed increases
(the group truth came in widespread change for the extreme
brown black temperatures out observing over the last 50 years

[a *convergent world*], and transformed the cold
days when i began gathering frost [global population peaks
in mid-century and declines thereafter] and looking back less
frequently to become heat waves everywhere with cold nights

at seven becoming more frequent [*rapid change*

in economic structures toward

by movement[115] known[116] and then[117] added[118] to substitution[119] calming[120] and violet[121] indigo[122] as the voiceless[123] approach[124]

a serv·ice and

in·formation

eco·nomy] and hot days while a white horse returns to non-car polar treatment [reductions in material intensity])

[115] a specific occupational strategy for articulation

(horses in unusually paleoclimate healing quickly suggest warmth likely around the last half century's time [a convergent world] and safety information during any other period [global population that peaks in mid-century and declines thereafter], and i was holding at least four narrow Toltec time helmets in the previous 1300 years with my present polar region arms significantly warmer last time [rapid change in economic structures toward a service and information economy] and ran for an extended period *lowering my polar ice volume [reductions in material intensity] and reductions in led to square the 125,000 year geometric direction of 4 to 6 meters of sea level [***introduction of***

clean*{producing relatively little pollution}* and resource *efficient {high ratio output to input}* technologies*] and an old 50-year opening likely to average Northern Hemisphere temperatures rather than stepping out of the last 500 years of running high in four 20th century directions [***emphasis is on global solutions to economic, social and environmental sustainability including***

improved equity*{residual{re*

maining{continue{exist{live} value}])

[116] discouraging governmental nativity

(while believing we finished walking around the average temperature increase, a very rapid economic growth came around the bend and gave a way to understanding the luminous grassy global ocean dog of at least 3000m based in a global meadow near population peak trees in mid-century beside the tall standing declines thereafter, however, several of the guy bears of depth stood directly on the horses absorbing the grazing path in order to initiate rapid introduction of new and more efficient technologies while we exited the mad climate system barn to add more than 80% heat to the growing convergence among regions, and said such contributing moments caused the warming sea level to expand inward, allowing capacity building to catch a flying ocean seawater wolf for increased cultural and social interactions concerning trees)

[117] the subjective lagging of events

(a group of six or seven mountain glacier palominos suddenly sprung the hemisphere bear microphone open to gather substantial reduction in regional differences in per capita incomes as well as a decline on average for exceeded flying on melting snow cover, fossil intensive, brown and black bear lands — a widespread decrease in deep organic glaciers for non-fossil energy sources and ice cap vines contributing to the accumulation and balance for not relying too heavily on one particular energy

source, and to cut polar bear snowfall in the delicate Greenland and Antarctic temple towards sea level rise in both grizzly and mammary for a very heterogeneous world, and for outlet glacier flow speeds to become self reliant in the preservation of local identities, thus exposing increases for some through losses due to hanging while fertility patterns across regions converge very slowly)

[118] regional inhabitations of the volatile

(persuading her horses to observe sea level increases as subsequent to the continuously increasing population, and hold high confidence in the panicked wolf of economic development which is primarily regionally oriented, yet as she recognized the rate of quickly unconscious people rising from the 19th to the 20th century as per capita economic growth, she ran for the safety, so as to stay looking at the truck slamming against the sum of an old wooden shed and a stitched tattoo with an arm's climate handle estimated knocking in the smaller, more narrowly observed sea level contributions at continental basin scales where tall technological change appears more fragmented and reserved in the numerous ocean climates governed by the long-term regional mustache doctor of slower comprehension])

[119] the referring mask of science

(ocean salinity changes inside the turning red sedan began flipping Arctic temperatures in widespread changes just i called her name due to heat drought intensity in a challenged convergent world with aspect wind patterns including wear waves to the extent of recognized so gone tropical cyclones dating back to the heavy

precipitation doctors struggling to free extreme weather into my arms within the ice examination tent of global population peak at mid-century and decline thereafter, and with the same surprise, she urged the average arctic temperatures to wear a claw when greeting the increasing yellow ball with almost twice the global average rate of rapid change in economic structures toward a service and information economy — closing the 100 year door to shrink the annual safety average by 2.7% recognized with the same surprise)

[120] reconstructing a branched interiority

(becoming bored by the hurried maximum precipitation area, an introduction of clean and resource efficient technologies was developed in the barn, one covering the Northern Hemisphere by light and decreasing seasonally out through the frozen tops of waiting ground, with the second generating emphasis on global solutions to economic growth, thus it observed closing the door to near transformation by about 7% down to one young, significant, curly haired bag woman in the eastern parts of North and South America pulling bears from northern Europe and increased places in central Asian while waiting to dry jeans with social and environmental sustainability, and just outside the Sahel with improved equity, southern Asia was observed waiting with southern African in the tent of Mediterranean walking without additional climate initiatives)

[121] affecting partial respiration

(walking mid-latitude while we understood that the emphasis is on local solutions to economic, social, and environmental

sustainability, we exited the barn while asking her westerly temperature condition to strengthened her luminous snow pack hemisphere in both wind grazing and continuously increasing global population areas, especially with snow cover since the 1960s when someone came in with intermediate levels of economic development and took the drying winds to change increased links with higher drought temperatures and less rapid, but more diverse technological changes, and having contributed in that, her precipitation wouldn't last near a decreased tall sea surface with tree links inside the meadow pattern drought tent which oriented toward environmental protection and social equity for all bears)

[122] an inflammation of earlier delineations

(the palomino group and their delicate truth came through in widespread change for the extreme brown black temperatures out observing over the last 50 years in a convergent mammary world, and transformed the injured cold days when i began gathering deep cut frost from the exposed global population peaks in mid-century and declines thereafter, which looking back less frequently, became hanging heat waves everywhere with cold nights at seven becoming more frequent, and spurring rapid change in economic structures toward a service and information economy, and hot days while a white horse returns to non-car polar treatment towards reductions in material intensity)

[123] all or part of

(persuading her horses in unusually paleoclimate healing to stay quickly suggested warmth likely around the last half century's time

of a convergent world where safety information during any other period, including global population that peaks in mid-century and declines thereafter, was stitched to looking and held at least four narrow Toltec time helmets in the previous 1300 years with my present polar region arms significantly warmer last time the doctor issued rapid change in economic structures toward a service and information economy, therefore running for an extended period and lowering my polar ice volume for reductions in material intensity, and reductions which led to square the 125,000 year geometric direction of 4 to 6 meters of sea level as an introduction of clean and resource efficient technologies where an old 50-year opening is likely to average Northern Hemisphere temperatures rather than stepping out of the last 500 years of running high in four 20th century directions where emphasis is on global solutions to economic, social and environmental sustainability including improved equity])

[124] included expressions of belonging to measurement

(exhausted and terrified while believing we finished walking a herd of wild mustangs across the average temperature increase, they came galloping from around the side of a very rapid economic growth running from a terrifying wolf predator which also came around the bend. the horses could usually outrun any other animal as a way to understanding, but this one was relentlessly luminous in its grassy global ocean, being directed by a government program of at least 3000m of rounded up wild horses from public lands. in the global meadow near target horses, there was a population peak of trees in mid-century northwestern

infinity[125]? **1.1.0.1.1.1.0.1.1.0.0.1.1.0.0.0.1.0
.1.1.0.0.0.1.1.0.1.0.0.1.0.1.1.0.0.1.0.0.1**

Colorado beside the tall standing declines, so the horses hit in a straightaway thereafter, however, several of the full stride guy bears of depth stood along a camouflaged fence directly across from the horses, while absorbing the gradually funneling and grazing path, in order to trap and initiate the rapid introduction of the roundup crew, and release new and more efficient technologies as a "Judas horse." while we exited the mad front pack of the climate system barn to add a lead mustang to the more than 80% heat within the tiny corral of the growing convergence among regions, the horses were screeching and said such contributing moments had piled up on top of causes for the warming sea level. the dust flew, to expand inward, and allowed a capacity for the gate to slam into the building in order to catch a flying wolf pulling away the ocean seawater wolf for increased horses in cultural and social interactions where there were concerns for the bears who were finishing trees)

[125] splendor flanking a depositing watermark

(few of the horses from a group of six were released back toward the seventh mountain glacier palomino when it suddenly came into range and sprung the hemisphere bear microphone to put up adoption of an opening to gather substantial reductions in the relocation of the regional differences in per capita government holding facilities for incomes as well as a large number of

.0.1.1.1.0.0.0.1.1.1.0.0.1.1.1.1.0.0.1.0.1.

0.1.1.0.0.0.1.1.1.0.1.1.0.1.1.1.0.1.1.0.0.1

.1.0.0.0.1.0.1.1.0.0.0.1.1.0.1.0.0.1.0.1.1

.0.0.1.0.0.1.0.1.1.1.0.0.0.1.1.1.0.0.1.1.1.

eligibilities declining on average for exceeding the selling to slaughterhouses while flying on melting snow cover. thanks to the bears, who would preserve fossil intensive brown and black bear passed laws for exclusive bear lands, there was a widespread decrease in banning the inhumane in deep organic glaciers for the treatment of wild horses and non-fossil energy sources, where ice safeguards had been put into place to cap vines contributing to the ability to sell for accumulation, and balance for not slaughtering or relying too heavily on one law in result of a particular energy source. a two-decades-long crusade to cut polar bear snowfall and the wild horses of the delicate Greenland and Antarctic gutted temple territory created leverage towards sea level rise for days before the holiday recess in both grizzly and mammary bears who were getting ready for a very heterogeneous world, and leaving for the long weekend in an outlet glacier flow where the final touches of speed had become self reliant to the rider in the preserving and the local removal of all identities, thus exposing increases for protections for wild horses through some losses due to burros

1.0.0.1.0.1.0.1.1.0.0.0.1.1.1.0.1.1.0.1.1.1
.0.1.1.0.0.1.1.0.0.0.1.0.1.1.0.0.0.1.1.0.1
.0.0.1.0.1.1.0.0.1.0.0.1.0.1.1.1.0.0.0.1.1
.1.0.0.1.1.1.1.0.0.1.0.1.0.1.1.0.0.0.1.1.1.
0.1.1.0.1.1.1.0.1.1.0.0.1.1.0.0.0.1.0.1.1.0
.0.0.1.1.0.1.0.0.1.0.1.1.0.0.1.0.0.1.0.1.1
.1.0.0.0.1.1.1.0.0.1.1.1.1.0.0.1.0.1.0.1.1.
0.0.0.1.1.1.0.1.1.0.1.1.1.0.1.1.0.0.1.1.0.0
.0.1.0.1.1.0.0.0.1.1.0.1.0.0.1.0.1.1.0.0.1
.0.0.1.0.1.1.1.0.0.0.1.1.1.0.0.1.1.1.1.0.0.
1.0.1.0.1.1.0.0.0.1.1.1.0.1.1.0.1.1.1.0.1.1
.0.0.1.1.0.0.0.1.0.1.1.0.0.0.1.1.0.1.0.0.1
.0.1.1.0.0.1.0.0.1.0.1.1.1.0.0.0.1.1.1.0.0
.1.1.1.1.0.0.1.0.1.0.1.1.0.0.0.1.1.1.0.0.0.
1.1.1.1.1.0.0.1.1.0.0.1.1.11.1.0.1.1.1.0.1.1

.0.0.1.1.0.0.0.1.0.1.1.0.0.0.1.1.0.1.0.0.1

.0.1.1.0.0.1.0.0.1.0.1.1.1.0.0.0.1.1.1.0.0.

1.1.1.1.0.0.1.0.1.0.1.1.0.0.0.1.1.1.0.1.1.1

.1.0.0.0.0.1.1.1.0.0.1.1.0.1.1.1.0.1.1.0.0

.1.1.0.0.0.1.0.1.1.0.0.0.1.1.0.1.0.0.1.0.1

.1.0.0.1.0.0.1.0.1.1.1.0.0.0.1.1.1.0.0.1.1.

1.1.1.1.0.1.1.1.0.1.1.0.0.1.1.0.0.0.1.0.1.1.

0.0.0.1.1.0.1.0.0.1.0.1.1.0.0.1.0.0.1.0.1.

1.1.0.0.0.1.1.1.0.0.1.1.1.1.0.0.1.0.1.0.1.1

.0.0.0.1.1.1.0.1.1.1.1.0.0.0.0.1.1.1.0.0.1.

1.1.0.1.1. If[126] the[127] center[128] gliding[129] is moving[130] at[131]

---

hanging, while fertility patterns across the over age regions converged very slowly and unsuccessfully)

[126] following ingenious selection

(adoption three times began persuading her horses to observe such animals in sea level increases as subsequent to the now sold and continuously increasing population, which without limitation and high confidence in auctions for the panicked wolf of economic

highest bidders for development, which is primarily oriented to regional local sale yards, thus she recognized other convenient livestock rates of quickly unconscious selling facilities for people rising from the 19th bear insertions to the 20th century as a one-page rider for per capita economic growth. consequently, she targeted budget-appropriations to run for safety, so that the bill on the eve would stay looking at a congressional deadline much like the truck slamming against the opportunity of the sum of an old wooden public shed and a stitched tattoo of legislative debate with an arm's climate handle. the following week, there was an estimated knocking in the smaller rider to uncover a more narrowly observed sea level, thanks in part to contributions at continental basin scales and a tip from the bears, where tall technological change appears in the printing office of more fragmented and reserved animal advocates for the numerous ocean climates governed by politicians from both the long-term regional mustache major parties and the outraged doctor of slower comprehension from the west])

[127] to retain numerous connotations

(so damaging to ocean salinity changes inside the bear amendment, she began turning the red sedan by beginning to flip as she passed on Arctic temperatures and widespread changes to an appropriations bill, but instead just called its name when no one knew about it due to the heat drought intensity in precisely the way a challenged convergent world of legislative process and aspect wind patterns would include the not working wear waves. yet, to the extent of the wolves motivations to recognize the so

gone tropical protection cyclones dating back to the bear ranchers of heavy precipitation and storm doctors struggling for leased lands of free extreme weather, the horses grazing along the arms of the ice examination, despite the protests of the global tent population which peaked to borrow at mid-century and declined thereafter, found imagery and ethos with the same surprise as an American cowboy urged to see the average arctic bear praised temperatures for wearing a claw and spurs when greeting the increasing yellow signature of the rider ball, with almost twice the legal global average rate of rapid capping series for changes in economic structures towards policy, the wolf moved toward a service and information economy with the government closing the 100 year door agency in charge of shrinking the annual safety management of horses by an average by 2.7%, which recognized the diminished with the same surprise of protected status)

[128] tropical figures considered equivalent

(the living symbols became bored by the hurried and historic maximum precipitation area, so an introduction of the pioneer spirit including clean and resource efficient western technologies was developed in the so called barn, one covering a northern rider causing hemisphere leaks by light and decreasing anger seasonally out through the frozen overwhelming tops of waiting ground, and the other with a bipartisan bill for the second generation emphasis on restoring global solutions to economic growth. the original intent was thus observed closing a similar amendment door to near transformation by stopping about 7% down to the one before its confirmation of youth, and the significant, curly haired bag

appropriations woman in the eastern part of the subcommittee for
North and South America pulling her jurisdiction over the bears
from northern Europe, so that all federal lands would increase
places in central Asia. with the bear as chairman, we waited
to dry jeans in the committee with social and environmental
sustainability, proving yet again that just outside the Sahel, there
was one horse who could improve equity in southern Asia and
make an observed difference while waiting with southern blocked
Africa in the tent of Mediterranean amendment walking without
additional climate going to vote on initiatives concerning the part
of the bears)

[129] overgrown institutional fetishes

(the responsible were walking mid-latitude while we understood
the administration of the horses where the emphasis was on
acres of public land indicating local solutions to economic, social,
historical, and environmental sustainability, so we exited to work
closely in the barn while asking the ranchers of the westerly
temperature condition to strengthen their commercial interests
in her luminous snow pack hemisphere around gas and oil in
both wind, grazing, coal, and timber industries to continuously
increase global population areas. the management was especially
concerned with snow cover since the use of these lands in the
1960s when someone came to oversee the wild in the intermediate
levels of horses as one economic development, and took the
small part of the drying winds to change increases in the bureau,
which does link higher drought temperatures with the general
public and less rapid, but more an emotional attachment to

diverse technological changes. yet, having one of its most valued contributions in precipitation, the important responsibilities would not last near a decreased celebration in film of tall sea surface with intricate tree literature links inside the meadow pattern of our nation's historical drought tent which oriented toward the mustangs, and environmental protection for social equity to help the wolves defend all bears completely)

[130] a densely contained interest

(the historic expedition of the palomino group and their open delicate truth came through in the frontier of widespread change for the extreme pulling of plowed brown black temperatures out observing the delivered mail over the last 50 years in carrying soldiers in a convergent mammary world, thus battling the transformed and injured cold summing up of days when she began gathering the feelings of many deep cut frosts from her speech, exposing the global population peaks in an overturn of the bear rider by mid-century and then declining thereafter. criticizing the bear's management and looking back less frequently, they became like the wild horses hanging in the heat waves everywhere with actions on cold nights at seven becoming taken more frequent, and spurring rapid movement, ensuring the proper change in economic structures toward an operation of the wild service and information economy. meanwhile, the horses endured hot days while in the program without resorting to the white horse return of non-car, slaughterhouse polar treatment towards the reduction in animal material intensity to drive up interest)

[131] confusing object actions

(the excess animals persuaded her horses in unusually removed paleoclimate healing situations to stay quickly abreast of the range of suggested warmth likely around the excessive last half century's time of the determined, convergent world, where safety in the interior of information during any other period would see threats including global population peaks and a thriving natural mid-century decline thereafter. the ecological balance was stitched up to look like a multiple-use relationship holding at least four narrow area Toltec time helmets in the rancher's previous 1300 years, with an amendment present for polar regional arms which significantly allowed warmer days the last time the doctor of mechanized roundups had issued a rapid change warning to the economic wolves and their trucks in structure towards a service and number information economy. therefore, the running of an increase in drama as an extended period and lowering more revisions for polar ice volume allowed for older reductions in material intensity, with a sick and lame reduction leading to a square longitude of animals to be destroyed in the 125,000 year geometric direction of the most humane 4 to 6 meters in the highest manner possible for sea level. as a measure of introduction for clean and resource airtight efficient technologies where an old population of 50-year openings is likely, the problems of the future are averaged to the Northern Hemisphere with temperature surges rather than dealing with stepping out of the problems of last 500 years in running on the range so high in their fourth 20th century. yet, to avoid the roundups and

the[132] speed[133] of[134] effortless[135] carriage[136] with a velocity[137] of[138] accounting[139] union[140], then[141] what[142] friction[143] quotient[144] of

> directions where emphasis is on the slaughterhouse horrors, the global solution to economic and social revisions were specified as environmental sustainability to include improved horse-adoption equity rather than a program to dispose of wild healthy excess animals])

[132] the lowering rank in discontinuity

> (within a population of someone wild wandering around a grassy bend, many of the horses had increased thousands of years while grazing among the woods, thus adding provisions spanning ice cores to the most important excesses of animals concerning anthropogenic greenhouse gas, so we walked along the removed range with markedly increasing rolling green hillside meadows being determined as a result of human activities, where the threat of luminous art in trees and the tall thriving natural ecological music festival had exceeded by far the fossil fuel balance and multiple-use occurring over the last 650,000 years — a relationship in that area with some horses' attendants which stood grazing during the natural mechanized roundups on the range where several disappearances were due primarily to camping that began to increase the dramatic tree to land-use changes)

[133] commissioned diminutive influences

> (old, sick, and lame wolves began a huge annual prowling, including smoking and carbon dioxide destruction around a group of six or seven larger concentrations of the most humane man

bears gathering during that period to create an airtight treatment for the last ten years by just foreseeing the population problems in the center of the pre-industrial glass house, where such problems ranging from growth-rate to atmospheric concentrations qualified as individual predictions since three thousand brown, black bear dollars of four horses each carried the carbon dioxide of 650,000 years to the gathering of grizzly bears for a per horse fee, resulting in fossil fuel use and the white treatment of polar methane sevens to exceed the last natural humane year range)

[134] a displaced establishment abdicating disorder

(the owners were given title to the average leading golden horses which jumped with limited panic at the global activities since 1750, and the one-year probationary period which had a net effect change of confidence intended to eliminate the very high human Duke as an economic incentive for ranchers very likely to have been appearing in large numbers to warm quickly during the industrial era, and sell horses as if to run a rate increase through a loophole of more than 10,000 years against the big driving unprecedented iron safety of an old wooden slaughterhouse conversation shed of ozone-forming chemicals, thus wanting to include the revisions of contributions to the largest narrow glass wild horse openings for any decade due to emissions loosing their protected status and the tall tropospheric ozone contact doors in the owner received titles of at least the last 200 years of implications)

[135] theoretical inheritance

(it became all too clear to a land-cover bloodhound turning

changes nearby in the installed pro-ranching respective surface
snow forcing albedo to adjust the lesser-known play black
carbon aerosol music to create a like-minded exertion shield and
deposition barrier, where on the interior, the bears called the
warming climate system unequivocal and instituted a fee-waiver
recognition program for the global wolf name and the most willing
glass cars running on air and ocean with at least 100 wild horses
in the widespread melting of snow and ice to get them for free,
telling me of the same rising million roundup sea level surprise
and singing increases of enthusiastically removing the average
temperatures from horses on the range)

[136] supplanting unusual technicalities

*(revealing how the ranchers hurried rank among the average
wolves to get around standing outside in the instrumental
record of the horse limit concerning small fragile global surface
temperature latches in dozens of individuals where the twelve
warmest vibrating barn years along the ranchers' power with other
linear pushes against the horse warming trend, they closed the
truck door to increase planning sales in content to nearly twice
that for the powers of attorney years waiting in the microphone
lock, and advocated slaughter in the gravely atmospheric water
vapour where everybody knew what was happening despite the
throaty upper troposphere bear voices that nobody will admit
carried long over land and ocean.)*

[137] maturity between phasing

*(securing an independent view while we finished believing the
average temperatures of nonpartisan reports showing an increase*

in understanding of the wild horses with the global ocean dog placed with at least 3000m below the guy bears, a depth which stands directly among hundreds on the absorbing path, so we exited the mad starvation climate system barn to add a year's dehydration to more than 80% of the heat, and said such probationary periods contribute significant momentary causes of warming sea level adoptions which expanded to catch a primarily flying ocean seawater ranching wolf)

[138] causing noted compliance

(selling thousands more, the mountain glacier palomino suddenly sprung from the slaughter after the hemisphere microphone opened, and declined to obtain a title for the average exceeded flying on the very design of melting snow cover, hence a widespread decrease in deep organic fee-waiver programs for glaciers and ice cap vines contributing to a prescription of accumulation and cut snowfall in the delicate commercially exploited Greenland and Antarctic temples towards sea level where wild horses rise in both mammary and outlet glaciers to fund the animal flow speeds, exposing increases for some through responses to abuses and losses due to the hanging federally judged rules)

[139] a pneumatic tool

(under abuses persuading her to observe sea level increases still being reported and held in high confidence per the wolf, she become internal and recognized the rate of unconscious people in a series of articles rising from the 19th to the 20th falsified recorded century so as to stay looking at the identified track and truck

slamming against the sum of the bureau officials stitched tattoo with an arm's climate selling horses to slaughter to handle the estimated knock in the smaller enlistment of friends observing sea level contributions at the continental basin relative to adopted scales, and observances in the numerous ocean climates circumvented by the long-term regional mustache doctor on a per-person limit)

[140] the cylindrical impacting of shape

(announcing additional regulations for ocean salinity changes inside the red sedan to protect the horses from the flipping Arctic temperatures in widespread changes including the checking due to heat drought intensity and aspect spot-checking of wind pattern slaughterhouses, and the wear waves to the now signed extent of so gone tropical cyclones backing an affidavit ensuring the heavy precipitation doctor's struggle against the intent to sell free extreme weather into my arms within the horses and ice examination tent, so she urged that processing the average arctic temperatures at claw length might influence the increasing yellow ball meetings concerning the worst global average rate, thus closing the addressing of abuses all along the 100 year door to shrink the bear announcements of an annual safety average by 2.7% per decade with no intent)

[141] lacking depth descendants

(with the bear as director becoming bored by the maximum precipitation area, one covering a northern built reputation on hemisphere and light for decreasing seasonal output through the frozen tops of favored mining in the waiting ground, they

observed near transformation by about 7% down to the drilling interests of one young, significant, curly haired bag woman in the east which had been a part of the North and South American pull on northern Europe to increase the center of controversy among places in central Asia where drying was just outside the Sahel, and the sworn testimony of southern Asia had observed the southern African tent of Mediterranean walking as public-lands chairman)

[142] depressive productions in hostility

(she encouraged the ranchers walking mid-latitude to ask the westerly temperature conditions to strengthen its own agency in both luminous snow pack hemispheres for wind grazing and snow, which unfortunately, failed in an effort to re-cover when someone came and took the drying interior winds of change to increase links with higher drought temperatures and grazing permits to contribute precipitation that wouldn't last nearly as long as a decrease in tall conservation groups of sea surface with tree links inside the meadow pattern drought tent without anything inappropriate)

[143] affluent religious landscaping

(the administration was rounding up the group truth which came with widespread change for the extreme brown record-setting black temperatures observed over the last 50 years, and threatened to transform inclusion to more than the cold days, when i began gathering frost and looking back at the stone monuments less frequently, but also include heat waves everywhere with permanent cold nights to the power of seven, thus there became more frequent hot days while a white horse optimistic[145] strength[146] would[147] equal[148] companioned[149] truth[150]?

1.1.0.1.1.1.0.1.1.0.0.1.1.0.0.0.1.0.1.1.0.0

constructed building returns to non-car polar treatment during another depression)

[144] rhythmic under-structures of maturity

(the wide main corridor of horses is unusual for paleoclimate healing and quickly suggests the warmth likely around the high ceilings of last half century's time and safety information during any other period, but the feeling was not safe, but instead small as i was holding at least four narrow Toltec time helmets in the back office from the previous 1300 years with my present polar region arms in landmarks significantly warmer since last time, and the running for an extended period to lower the round table of my polar ice volume to reductions in led squared with the deputy assistant director of the 125,000 year geometric direction of 4 to 6 meters of renewable sea level resources had an old 50-year opening likely to average Northern Hemisphere planning operation temperatures rather than stepping out of the last 500 years as spokesperson for the four 20th century directions indicating numbers on their chart)

[145] flowing youth to shroud anxiety

(walking around a fiery activist, a luminous grassy meadow became ready to jump to the next task near a tall stand of trees

.0.1.1.0.1.0.0.1.0.1.1.0.0.1.0.0.1.0.1.1.1.

0.0.0.1.1.1.0.0.1.1.1.1.0.0.1.0.1.0.1.1.0.

0.0.1.1.1.0.0.0.1.1.1.1.1.0.0.1.1.0.0.1.1.1

1.1.0.1.1.1.0.1.1.0.0.1.1.0.0.0.1.0.1.1.0.0

resting on a sawhorse — several of us began volunteering like horses grazing)

[146] disputing civilized excursions

(as president to a group of six or seven bears gathered in the center, she was featured in countless newspaper articles with brown bears, black bears, grizzly bears, white polar bears who had all contracted severe cases of polio)

[147] extreme declarations

(undergoing an experimental operation, the horses panicked and were hospitalized for nearly nine months while we quickly ran along with the rest of the herd for the safety of an old wooden shed, all narrow, tall, and disfigured from the trauma)

[148] the abrupt resemblance

(turning just to take care of the animals, i called her name and recognized a truck pulling a livestock trailer, and with the same surprise saw blood dripping out of the back)

[149] acute combinations in restlessness

(as i hurried into the barn, it was jam-packed with all the others, and when closing the door, something was trampled under their feet while awaiting the bear)

.0.1.1.0.1.1.0.1.1.1.0.1.1.0.0.1.1.0.0.0.1.
0.1.1.0.0.0.1.1.0.1.0.0.1.0.1.1.0.0.1.0.0.
1.0.1.1.1.0.0.0.1.1.1.0.0.1.1.1.1.0.0.1.0.1
.0.1.1.0.0.0.1.1.1.0.0.0.1.1.1.1.1.0.0.1.1.
0.0.1.1.11.1.0.1.1.1.0.1.1.0.0.1.1.0.0.0.1.
0.1.1.0.0.0.1.1.0.1.0.0.1.0.1.1.0.0.1.0.0.
1.0.1.1.1.0.0.0.1.1.1.0.0.1.1.1.1.0.0.1.0.1
.0.1.1.0.0.0.1.1.1.0.1.1.1.1.0.0.0.0.1.1.1.
0.0.1.1.0.1.1.1.0.1.1.0.0.1.1.0.0.0.1.0.1.1
.0.0.0.1.1.0.1.0.0.1.0.1.1.0.0.1.0.0.1.0.1
.1.1.0.0.0.1.1.1.0.0.1.1.1.1.1.0.0.1.0.1.1.
0.0.1.0.0.1.0.1.1.1.0.0.0.1.1.1.0.0.1.1.1.1
.0.0.1.0.1.0.1.1.0.0.0.1.1.1.0.1.1.1.1.0.0.
0.0.1.1.1.0.0.1.1.0.1.1.1.0.1.1.0.0.1.1.0.0
.0.1.0.1.1.0.0.0.1.1.0.1.0.0.1.0.1.1.0.0.1.

0.0.1.0.1.1.1.0.0.0.1.1.1.0.0.1.1.1.1.1.1.0
.1.1.1.0.1.1.0.0.1.1.0.0.0.1.0.1.1.0.0.0.1.
1.0.1.0.0.1.0.1.1.0.0.1.0.0.1.0.1.1.1.0.0.
0.1.1.1.0.0.1.1.1.1.0.0.1.0.1.0.1.1.0.0.0.1
.1.1.0.0.0.1.1.1.1.1.0.0.1.1.0.0.1.1.11.1.0
.1.1.1.0.1.1.0.0.1.1.0.0.0.1.0.1.1.0.0.0.1.
1.0.1.0.0.1.0.1.1.0.0.1.0.0.1.0.1.1.1.0.0.
0.1.1.1.0.0.1.1.1.1.0.0.1.0.1.0.1.1.0.0.0.1
.1.1.0.1.1.1.1.0.0.0.0.1.1.1.0.0.1.1.0.1.1.1
.0.1.1.0.0.1.1.0.0.0.1.0.1.1.0.0.0.1.1.0.1
.0.0.1.0.1.1.0.0.1.0.0.1.0.1.1.1.0.0.0.1.1
.1.0.0.1.1.1.1.0.0.1.0.1.0.1.1.0.0.0.1.1.1.
0.1.1.1.0.0.0.1.1.1.0.0.1.11.1.0.1.1.1.0.1.1
.0.0.1.1.0.0.0.1.0.1.1.0.0.0.1.1.0.1.0.0.1
.0.1.1.0.0.1.0.0.1.0.1.1.1.0.0.0.1.1.1.0.0.

1.1.1.1.0.0.1.0.1.0.1.1.0.0.0.1.1.1.0.0.0.1
.1.1.0.0.0.1.11.1.0.1.1.1.0.1.1.0.0.1.1.0.0
.0.1.0.1.1.0.0.0.1.1.0.1.0.0.1.0.1.1.0.0.1.
0.0.1.0.1.1.1.0.0.0.1.1.1.0.0.1.1.1.1.0.0.1
.0.1.0.1.1.0.0.0.1.1.1.0.1.1.1.1.1.1.0.0.1.1
.0.0.0.1.1.0.1.1.1.0.1.1.0.0.1.1.0.0.0.1.0.
1.1.0.0.0.1.1.0.1.0.0.1.0.1.1.0.0.1.0.0.1.
0.1.1.1.0.0.0.1.1.1.0.0.1.1.1.1.0.0.1.0.1.0
.1.1.0.0.0.1.1.1.0.0.0.1.1.1.1.1.0.0.1.1.0.
0.1.1.11.1.0.1.1.1.0.1.1.0.0.1.1.0.0.0.1.0.
1.1.0.0.0.1.1.0.1.0.0.1.0.1.1.0.0.1.0.0.1.
0.1.1.1.0.0.0.1.1.1.0.0.1.1.1.1.0.0.1.0.1.0
.1.1.0.0.0.1.1.1.0.1.1.1.1.0.0.0.0.1.1.1.0.
0.1.1.0.1.1.1.0.1.1.0.0.1.1.0.0.0.1.0.1.1.0
.0.0.1.1.0.1.0.0.1.0.1.1.0.0.1.0.0.1.0.1.1.

1.0.0.0.1.1.1.0.0.1.1.1.1.0.0.1.0.1.0.1.1.0

.0.0.1.1.1.0.1.1.1.0.0.0.1.1.1.0.0.1.11.1.0

.1.1.1.0.1.1.0.0.1.1.0.0.0.1.0.1.1..1.0.0.1

.0.1.1.0.0.1.0.0.1.0.1.1.1.0.0.0.1.1.1.0.0.

1.1.1.1.0.0.1.0.1.0.1.1.0.0.0.1.1.1.0.1.1.1.

1.1.1.0.0.1.1.0.0.0. When[151] strength[152] posturing[153] approaches[154] infinity[155], what[156] value[157] equals[158] radiant[159] .

---

[150] positional designation of meaning

(while next to a holding pen, we understood the bears might unlock the trailer gate, so we untangled and scrambled to exit the barn)

[151] loyal theoretical assumptions

(falling over the trailer's edge, battered and bloody, the palomino was injured and landed on top of a deep cut through a delicate mammary with wide swaths of flesh torn from her exposed hanging sides)

[152] the example of intended action

(persuading her to stay pulled off her feet, and looking trampled to death, the stitched doctor was dragged up a ramp)

[153] resisting to continue argument

(inside a red sedan to speak before a committee, the doctor had a reputation as a horse advocate, and she urged that any attempt

by the bears to ridicule would be examined and closed outside the door for safety)

[154] departing characteristics in government

(becoming bored waiting for regular death threats, she transformed as a result of her activism into a young curly woman challenging walks through unregulated commercial exploitation, unregulated commercial exploitation ... ...

....

... .

[155] maintaining occupation by force

cut, cut, cut, cut, cut, cut, cut, cut, cut, cut, cut, cut,

cut, cut, cut, cut, Cut!!!

_____
_____
_____

restraint[160] plus[161] clear[162] maturation[163] when[164] divided[165] by[166] departures[167] potential[168]?

---

[156] the reflexivity of example

([all parties, taking into account their common but differentiated responsibilities{Kyoto 10}] asked her to stay, and said that if she continued, she wouldn't last another hour [in order to achieve sustainable development{Kyoto 10}] in that condition)

[157] gaining possession

(understanding the truth, [programmes to improve the quality of local emissions factors{Kyoto 10}] transformed back into a horse and [periodic updating of national inventories of anthropogenic emissions{Kyoto 10}]} returned to the car for treatment)

[158] persisting designation

(in order for the healing to truly occur, the four Toltec time travelers with helmets displaying [programmes containing measures to mitigate climate change{Kyoto 10}] ran in four directions, back through time with [measures to facilitate adequate adaptation to climate change{Kyoto 10}])

[159] resistance to withhold

(there was someone wandering among [the energy, transport and industry sectors as well as agriculture, forestry and waste management{Kyoto 10}] of the woods)

[160] persistent profiteering

(a huge prowling wolf of [national communications — programmes which contain measures that contribute to addressing climate change and its adverse impacts{Kyoto 10}] appeared just outside the glass house)

[161] the obstruction gaining

(the golden bloodhound's [promotion of effective modalities for the development, application and diffusion of ... environmentally sound technologies, know-how, practices and processes pertinent to climate change{Kyoto 10}] jumped up against the iron and glass door)

[162] revealing controlled advantages

(trying to [cooperate in scientific and technical research, promote the maintenance and the development of systematic observation systems, and develop data archives to reduce uncertainties related to the climate system{Kyoto 10}] the dog tried to shield the [strengthening of endogenous capacities and capabilities to participate in international and intergovernmental efforts{Kyoto 10}] between the wolf and me)

[163] accustomed positions in applicable truth

(the small fragile latch was vibrating to [cooperate in and promote at the international level, ... the development and implementation of education and training programs{Kyoto 10}] and the door lock strained as the wolf began to [train experts in this field, particularly for developing countries{Kyoto 10}])

[164] formal inheritance of legal dominion

(believing that it would [facilitate at the national level public awareness of, and public access to information on, climate change{Kyoto 10}], i stood directly behind the golden bloodhound *in the path of the opening door to catch [national communications information on programmes and activities pursuant to {the Kyoto Protocol}{Kyoto 10}])*

[165] an indicator of alliance

(the door suddenly sprung open: [1) the earth is warming; 2) human activity is largely to blame; and 3) the warming trend is likely to accelerate in the years ahead{GGUSA-GCI02 1}] and the wolf came flying towards me — [implications are profound and will affect fundamental human survival needs{GGUSA-GCI02 1}])

[166] bonded itinerate forces

(i held [floods, drought and the spread of infectious diseases like malaria{GGUSA-GCI02 2}] in my arms and was slamming them against the floor of [new regions {that} will put food, water, and public health resources under severe stress{GGUSA-GCI02 2}] and knocking unconscious [much of the world's forest {which} will die off from the stresses of drought, disease and insect attacks{GGUSA-GCI02 2}])

[167] the satirical persistence of ruling

(struggling to [expresses disappointment in their ... abandonment of the Kyoto Protocol{GGUSA-GCI02 2}], the wolf began to flip, transform in my arms — ["this is an area where the United States could be a leader..."{GGUSA-GCI02 2}])

[168] literary abstraction structuring determination

(there was a light coming down upon [the industrialized nations who are responsible for the majority of greenhouse gas ... who should bear the most responsibility{GGUSA-GCI02 2}] and visible through the tops of the trees was [the US {which} uses 25% of the world's energy resources{.ibid} — ["an area where the United States could be a leader..."{.ibid}] — [of the world's energy resources{.ibid} {.ibid {.i bid {i bid i bid .i bid

Director's Notes

LANGUISHING THE LANGUISHED

    Up and to the left
the points role underneath projecting where the rolling stack is standing within the tube of a collapsed diagonal.
    Up and to the right
the folder standing hollows a parallel flare engulfing the being turns and crumpled openings tape a secure binding of discarded planes.
    Up and to the left
the tree upon the top of a horned speaker provides a circular roll as growth languishes to turn flattering triangular camps once allegorical.
    Up and to the right
the destination disconnects a sound holder due to an impartial accounting of the subjective meaning past and the abstract.
    projecting the points in collapsing the collapsed, collapsing the collapsing for collapsing the rolling, rolling the engulfed in engulfing the hollow, a hollow to discard in the discarding of discards, discarding the opening for an opening to provide, providing horn in the horn of horning, the horn of flattering for a horn of languish, flattering their languishing in languishing the languished, languishing the disconnect for disconnecting destination, destination of disconnecting in disconnecting disconnection, a subjecting disconnection for a subjecting accounting, the subjecting to account with an end in sight.

Epilogue

A Portent Pie Singing

Five and twenty portents draining from. Five and twenty from draining away portents. Five and twenty draining portents from a pie. Five and twenty portending to drain a pie. Five and twenty pies draining away. Five and twenty draining pies portend away. Five and twenty away pies portending from. Five and twenty from away draining portending pies. Five and twenty pies draining away from imperialism. Five and twenty portents imperializing

FROM DRAINING PIES. FIVE AND TWENTY DRAINING IMPERIALS FROM PORTENT. FIVE AND TWENTY IMPERIALS PORTEND DRAINING. FIVE AND TWENTY PORTENDING IMPERIALS DRAIN FROM AWAY. FIVE AND TWENTY IMPERIALS PORTENDING TO DRAIN. FIVE AND TWENTY IMPERIAL PIES DRAINING PORTENTS. FIVE AND TWENTY PIES FROM DRAINED IMPERIALS PORTENDING AWAY. FIVE AND TWENTY DRAIN FROM IMPERIALIZING PIES. FIVE AND TWENTY IMPERIAL PIES DRAIN SINGING PORTENT. FIVE AND TWENTY DRAIN SINGING FROM IMPERIALIZED PORTENT. FIVE AND TWENTY PORTENTS SINGING AWAY IMPERIALISM. FIVE AND TWENTY PIES SING PORTENDING IMPERIALS AWAY. FIVE AND TWENTY SINGING

AWAY FROM IMPERIAL DRAINS. FIVE AND TWENTY DRAIN SINGING PIES IN IMPERIALISM. FIVE AND TWENTY PORTENTS DRAINING IMPERIALISM FROM PIES. FIVE AND TWENTY SING DRAINING PIES AWAY FROM IMPERIALISM. FIVE AND TWENTY SINGING IMPERIALS DRAIN PIES AWAY. FIVE AND TWENTY DRAINS SINGING PIES FROM BLOOMING. FIVE AND TWENTY BLOOMING IMPERIAL PIES DRAIN AWAY FROM SINGING. FIVE AND TWENTY PIES SINGING BLOOMS FROM DRAINING PORTENTS. FIVE AND TWENTY IMPERIALIZING PIE BLOOMS DRAIN AWAY FROM PORTENDED SINGING. FIVE AND TWENTY PORTENDING BLOOMS DRAINING FROM IMPERIALS. FIVE AND TWENTY DRAIN A SINGING BLOOMING PIE

IN IMPERIALIZING PORTENT. FIVE AND TWENTY BLOOMING PORTENTS DRAINING FROM SINGING PIES. FIVE AND TWENTY IMPERIALISTS SINGING DRAIN THE PORTENTS OF BLOOMING PIES. FIVE AND TWENTY SINGING PIES BLOOM THE PORTENTS OF DRAINING IMPERIALISM. FIVE AND TWENTY IMPERIALISTS DRAIN SINGING BLOOMS WITH PORTENT. FIVE AND TWENTY SINGING PORTENTS BLOOM FROM IMPERIAL PIES. FIVE AND TWENTY IMPERIAL BLOOMS DRAIN SINGING PIES WITH PORTENT. FIVE AND TWENTY IMPERIAL PIES DRAINED AWAY IN BLOOMING PORTENT FROM NEUTRALIZED SINGING.

Posterior Technical

VENTURE II ..

75. 180 round 5.56mm magazines
76. ammunition for satisfying conservation goals
77. AC-130 Spectre gunship to increase slenderness
    a. aligning resting absolutions
        i. we were in a country setting working with a group of people.
    b. the reconsidered notion of course
        i. i had a new job in service waiting for guests to arrive.
78. acetaminophen tablets for narrow band coloring
79. adhesive bandage for speculative investments
80. Airborne Radio System to control hormone fluctuations
81. ammonia inhalant solution aromatic ampoules to ease appearances
82. Amphibious Assault Vehicle (AAV) to smooth floral ornamentation

- a. the degree of aggression
  - i. there were very large wolves that periodically ran through the camp.
    - 1. everyone ran for safety
- b. memory aggravating the plot
  - i. if anyone was caught by surprise, they had to stand very still.
    - 1. the wolf will not notice and pass by.
83. antibiotics to conduct selective worship
84. Armored Personnel Carrier (APC) for stylish blunders
85. atropine injection for continuous movement
86. ballistics for characteristic flowering
87. bandage scissors to ease structural imbalances
    - a. the application of memory
      - i. out in the open forest
        - 1. we stood very still while it sniffed us.
        - 2. the wolf continued on its way through the trees.
    - b. preservation of intent

        i. as if the wolf might have been hunting.
88. bayonet to process separation activities
89. biological warfare antidotes for rapid instrument monitoring
    a. questions of past history
        i. it wasn't clear if the wolf was simply passing through.
        i. ferociousness
    b. evident behavior
        i. there was an aggressive sense about the wolf.
        i. desperate, but focused
        ii. its pursuit
90. blood bandages for dimensional imaging
91. Blue Force Tracker for alphanumeric logo editing
92. burn dressings to document sentience
93. calamine lotion for empty holographic spaces
94. canteen to preserve satire
    a. anticipating habit
        i. i began to feel threatened as if i was in danger.
        i. causing the wolf to attack

95. casualties for patterned language discrepancies
96. category five hurricanes to station informal dissonance
97. catheter for addressing translations
98. CH-46E Sea Knight helicopter for ambient noise control
    a. relevant mirroring
        i. we ran inside a big canvas hunting tent.
    b. contained memorization
        i. a mess tent for feeding
99. CH-53E Super Stallion helicopter for aromatic foliage fertilization
100. chapstick to moralize degree principles
    a. vertical axis
        i. the tent collapsed and we were left huddled.
101. chemical warfare antidotes for stubborn complacency
102. Combat Search and Rescue (CSAR) to minimize amusement
103. continuous heat waves to activate social capital
104. cough drops for tenacity of purpose
    a. relative venting
        i. no longer any air

                            1.   there was just
                                   a thin layer of
                                      canvas.
                    b.   exhaustive determining
                            1.   barrier between us
                                1. the forest
    105.   decontamination kit for
                         reckless arrogance
    106.   devastating tornados to
                          design memoranda
    107.   diazepam injection for
                         textured anxieties
    108.   drought, disease and insect
             attacks for representative
                 portfolio development
    109.   Enhanced Position Location
             Reporting System for measuring
                         private property
    110.   Tri-Fold Shovel for custom
                         ceremonial passages
                    a.   aggravated gardening
                            1.   we believed that the
                            wolves could still smell
                                       us.
                                1.   as if we were
                    b.   imagining architectures
                            1.   we could no longer
                            see outside the tent.
                                1.   know the wolves
    111.   Expeditionary Fighting
             Vehicle (EFV) for overcrowding

112. extreme magnitude earthquakes for poignant memory reflections
113. extrication resources for ambiguous grammar
114. eye drops for rhetorical developments
    a. resolute ambitions
        i. to remain paralyzed
            1. fear
115. wind, water, and solar power for plural relationship constructions
116. F-35 Joint Strike Fighter for suggestive dreaming
117. field dressing to exhibit wholeness
118. first aid pouch for elemental surveys
    a. descriptive allocations
        i. the unknown
            1. the wolves might
    b. latency issues
        i. any time
119. foot powder for undeveloped pragmatism
120. fragmentation for compressed insults
121. GPS navigation system for incubation activities
    a. horizontal shift
        i. tent at this point
            1. more dangerous even

  b. lengthening refractions
    i. we couldn't move because we couldn't see.
      1. wolves
122. grenade for developing recordable investment actions
123. H-92 Super Hawk helicopter for cultivated branch exchanges
124. helmet for colloquial adaptations
125. High-Mobility Multipurpose Wheeled Vehicle (Humvee) for tapering hesitation
  a. desiring sight
    i. in the country
      1. i am traveling with a large Swedish family.
  b. extroverted darkness
    i. returning home
      1. i offer to pay for my accommodation
126. clean and efficient technologies for percussive formations
127. insect sting treatment at temperate extensions
128. intense acidification of the ocean for sub-visceral conversations
129. Iridium satellite phones for poetic insight
  a. delicate reverence

       i. work done
          1. there was no cost in addition to the trade for lodging.
  b. forward tendencies
       i. reluctantly accepting the gift
          1. he gave me two turquoise knobs.
  c. prescribed dreaming
       i. there were square pieces of stone embedded inside and outside.
          1. mosaic

130. Light Armored Vehicle (LAV) to specify resemblances
131. Line-of-sight communications systems to legislate adjournment
132. waste recycling and composting for pejorative terminologies
133. M16A2 5.56mm Rifle for disagreeable intensity
134. M1A1 Abrams tank to distress applications
  a. pacifying temperance
       i. he rested his head on my knee.
       i. to stroke his forehead gently
  b. established peace
       i. the woman came in and approached us.

        i. collecting the bits of turquoise
135. Marine Expeditionary Family of Fighting Vehicles (MEFFV) for lengthening astute legacies
136. Medium Tactical Vehicle Replacement (MTVR) to relate organism control
    a. memorable invocation
        i. i quickly put them in my pocket so she wouldn't take them.
        i. smiling, she welcomed me home.
137. intergovernmental cooperation for constituting prophesy
138. MH-60S Knight Hawk for prophetic significance
139. Mobile Subscriber Equipment for chemical entry diversification
    a. parallel ambitions
        i. i suddenly realized that i was from there.
        i. deciding to stay and continue traveling
    b. recalling destinations
        i. a woman was standing by the side of the road.
        i. a red native scarf

140. Mounted Digital Automated Communications Terminal (MDACT) to hold investment language
141. MV-22s Ospreys helicopter for characterizing related absorption polices
142. nail clippers for peripheral compositions
    a. compatible equivalents
        i. looking like
            1. she was delighted with my decision to stay.
    b. grammatical designations
        i. dark vermilion carpet
            1. several of us were sitting together.
143. increased social equity for hereditary engagements
144. oxygen generator for fluency
145. pharyngeal airway for religious burrowing
146. pistol belt to refract surface tensions
147. massive refugee migrations to obstruct networking
    a. relational consonants
        i. spilling some wine
            1. i immediately wiped it up to avoid a stain.
    b. nascent concordance

        i. to withstand
            1. imagining that the color was chosen

148. protective mask for intense anguish
149. ready-to-eat meal (MRE) for diminutive constitutions
150. rifle for optically distant distributions
    a. ancestral assumptions
        i. speaking French
            1. she remembered the necessity of learning.
151. SH-60 Sea Hawk to engage precipitated transport
152. severe typhoons for organic taxonomy engagements
153. Single Channel Ground Radio System for mystic lyricism
154. sinus tablets for ethereal anecdotes
    a. characteristic anxieties
        i. kissing me
            1. we were alone — something very sweet between us.
    b. pressing specifications
        i. looking up sweetly
            1. he buried his face in my stomach.
155. small arms for petty procedures

156. snake bite kit to legislate variability
157. splint for proclaiming destructive persistence
   a. diminutive temporalities
      i. my left breast
         1. what would happen if we had children?
   b. textural inclinations
      i. such beauty
         1. implying how they would be
158. Stryker Armored Vehicles for curtailing surface spectacles
159. sunscreen for authoritative flexibility
160. environmental preservation and sustainability for identity
161. suspenders to arouse suspicion
   a. extraordinary rapture
      i. running
         1. several of the teammates were there waiting for him.
   b. signifying dependence
      i. becoming unavailable
         1. he was distracted and dealing with the situation.
162. toilet articles for varied living industries
163. towel for meditation

164. tsunamis for universal phrase shifting
 a. limiting methodology
  i. attention
   1. i sensed that they knew we were there.
 b. theoretical histories
  i. they were building a huge fire with stacks of timber.
  i. like a wall of flames several feet high
165. tweezers for discrete plumage
166. vaccines to encase exploits
167. waterproof bag for recording sanctuary pursuits

End Notes

226. The elements are aspected by a courteous gaze through which the **ambiguity of material** respectability is concerned with only the lightest announcement of **active mood and experimentation**.

227. Shifting metaphor underfoot creates a softness through swelling that is often generated by the wide sweeping evaluations to the left and expressed through structure.

228. Gravity is paramount in the organization

OF ANGELS WHERE NOTHING ATTEMPTS TO CONCERN THE TOOL AND

MATERIAL FOR DISCOVERING SYNTHESIZED INDENTATIONS OF A MORE

229. DRASTICALLY OBSERVED TYPE. **THE FEATURES ARE MUSCULAR IN CONCENTRATION WITH MEAGER SUBLIMATED PROCESSES CHARACTERISTIC OF TYPICAL EXISTENCE OUTSIDE THE RELATIONSHIP TO THEIR PARTICULAR NEUTRALIZING EFFECTS ON VOLUME.**

230. MOVING PHENOMENA OFTEN CRYSTALLIZE SUCH DEMATERIALIZED EFFORTS THROUGH ADAPTATION TO QUALITY IMITATIONS AND ARE SURE TO EXHIBIT TINY DROPS OF EXTENSION WHERE THE FORMING CASCADES SURGE ONWARD THROUGH MODULATION.

231. ONE FINDS A REDISCOVERY OF A THOUSAND SCULPTORS EVALUATING THE PORTRAIT CONSCI

OUS CONVEXITIES

OF GRACEFUL SYMMETRIES

AS THEIR SUBTLE ARTICULATION OF BONES ARE

232. ACCUSTOMED TO PLASTIC SURFACES FAR AND WIDE. SHE WORKS WITH THE GENESIS OF STAGES INDICATING A KINETIC EASEL LEGIBLE THROUGH SIMILAR TENDENCIES WEDGED IN ADVANCED POSITIONS WHERE A RATHER FLAT CULTURAL MASS IS ORGANIC YET GRACEFUL IN ITS DISCOVERY OF A TWISTED GRASP.

233. THE BLOCKED-OUT DEVELOPMENT

OF GASEOUS EXPLOITATION IS ONCE BROKEN

AND THEN REUNITED WITHIN THE PHOTOGRAPHIC

PROTRUSIONS THAT MATTER TO THE

NONLINEAR AFFIRMATIONS OF COLOR AND THE BASIS OF

DEEPER MODULATION.

234. MONUMENTAL CONFIGURATIONS
OF TEXTURAL STUDY MOVING PERFECTLY THROUGH THE
PREDECESSORS OF AN ALMOST NEGATIVE POLE OF NON-
GEOMETRIC VITALITY SINGLED THROUGH RELIEF

AND **EARLY**

SALIENCY
TO UNTOUCHED DOCUMENTS OF CRYSTALLINE PRISMS.

235. THE REJECTED DISTINCTION IN MATTER RELATES TO OUR

UNDERSTANDING OF PERSISTED

VOLUME WHEN

INITIATING A RENDERING OF MOTION TOWARDS AN

236. INGENIOUS RELATIVE SHADOW.

THE PIGMENTS EXPLORED THROUGH IMITATIVE EMPHASIS **ARE** SHADOWED BY A FUNDAMENTAL PRE-RENAISSANCE PERIOD OF NATURALISTIC VALUES AND CONTEMPORARY ARTISTIC LIGHT.

237. A RETROSPECT OF ETERNAL

DEFINITIONS SHOWS MASTERY OF THE FREE TASK OF EMPHASIZING PLASTIC CHISEL-CUT CAUTIONS DIVERSIFIED AND SEEN BY A MAN EXPLORING THE USE OF SHADOWS AND

ESTHETICS TO OUTGROW HER RICH CONTEMPLATION.

238. THE MORE DYNAMIC CONCEPT OF BLURRING AN APPROACH NOT ONLY DEFINES THE VALUES OF SOLIDS, BUT CONSTITUTES THE INFLUENCE OF SIMILAR WORK BY ATTEMPTING THE PREDECESSORS OF

TOOL

AND MASTERY.

239. A PHOTOGRAPHERS SEQUENCE OF MANY IS CONTAINED WITHIN THE TEMPTING LOCATION OF SUBJECT AND ENCOUNTER PRODUCING THE INTIMATE AND IMPLICIT INTEREST IN ORGANIZATION.

240. THE PORTRAIT APPEARS SPONTANEOUS IN TAKING THE SUBJECT RELATIVE TO THE TENDERED MATERIALS OF EXAMPLE AND FRAGMENTATION.

241. POSSIBLE DEMONSTRATIONS ACT AS HORIZONTAL WORKINGS TO IMITATE THE TYPES OF METHODOLOGIES BECOMING MOVEMENT AND DISCIPLINE.

242. THE UNPROBLEMATIC PRODUCTION OF ANTHROPOLOGY IS VISIBLE ABOVE THE IMAGE OF DISTRESS SUGGESTED BY THE WORK LOCATED ALONG RELATIVE TYPES.

243. THE ENCOUNTERS OF VISUAL FRONTIERS HAS FORMED A WORKING SUBJECT UNIQUE TO LANDSCAPES AND FILM SUFFUSED WITH AN UNPRECEDENTED KNOWLEDGE OF **244.** BOUNDARY. THE CULTURES OF UNIQUE WITNESSING ARE SUPERSEDED BY THE TRACEABLE AND CLEAR POSTURES OF ILLUSTRATIONS NECESSARILY COLORED BY EXPECTATION AND TRAVEL.

245. SOCIETY CARRIES EXPECTED IDENTITY EXPLICITLY COMPARED TO REQUIRED HISTORIES CREATED TO TRACE RESEARCH AND EMPATHY.

246. THE UNITED MEMORY OF READING ORIGINS AS UNCONDITIONALLY ACCEPTED WITHOUT AN AUDIENCE CONSIDERS CHARACTER WITHOUT UNDERSTANDING VANITY AND ARROGANCE.

247. RETURNING TO DEDICATION AND THE NATURAL JUDGE OF STUDENT AND SCHOOL RELIEVES THE ASHES OF POWER AND CONTROL AND MEDIATES THE REBIRTH OF NOTHING ARTIFICIAL.

248. THEIR INSTITUTIONS NATURALLY MAINTAIN OBSCURE CARE AND FUNCTION IN ORDER TO EXIST AS SPECTACLE RATHER THAN UNFOLDING THEIR INCRIMINATION.

249. TO ORIGINATE IN TRUE WONDER OF BEAUTY AND THE MEANING OF RESPECT IS TO INSPIRE AN ORIGINATED RESISTANCE TO THE STORM OF ESCAPE.

250. THE REDEEMED CONTRADICTION FORETELLS OF THE DIGNITY INVOKED BY WISDOM AND A MENTAL UNIFICATION OF IMAGE AND FUTURE.

251. PRIMARY INSPIRATION IN **CULTURE AND DISCOVERY** ARE OPPOSED TO ACKNOWLEDGED OPPRESSION AND THE SIGNS OF RELATIONAL DOMINATION. **252.** THE AUDIENCE OF FRONTIERS IS DOCUMENTED AND **TRANSACTED** WITHOUT PREVIOUS **RELATIONSHIP** TO CULTURE AND PRESENTED AS ANYTHING BUT **COLONIAL**.

253. ASSESSMENT AND CONSOLIDATION ARE OBSERVED IN LANGUAGES PRECEDING THE APPOINTMENT OF **UNMAPPED HISTORICAL FRAMEWORKS** WHERE PERSONAL JOURNEYS ARE CONCERNED.

254. INTIMATED INTELLIGENCE REDEFINES SPEECH CONCERNING THE CONTEMPORARY FASCINATION WITH RELIGION AND **ARTIFACT** EMPLOYED IN DISTINGUISHING DIFFERENCE.

255. A region becoming natural IN RESEARCH AND PUBLICATION UNDERTAKES AN IMPORTANT INTERPRETATION WITH SERIOUS EXPERIENCE AND AMUSEMENT. **256.** REMARKABLE VISIBILITY IS SELECTED FROM THE PRESENT COLLECTION OF EMPIRE AND ARCHIVE RELATING TO ORAL HISTORIES AND FUNDAMENTAL INTERPRETATIONS OF TENSION.

WORKS CITED

Intergovernmental Panel on Climate Change.
"Climate Change 2007: The Physical Science Basis (Summary for Policymakers)." February 2007. <http://media.washingtonpost.com/wp-srv/nation/documents/climate_report_020207.pdf>.

Global Green USA & Green Cross International.
"Confronting Climate Change: Averting a Global Environmental Crisis (Policy Report)." March 2002.
<http://www.globalgreen.org/media/climate/ClimatePolicyReport.pdf>.

United Nations.
"Kyoto Protocol to the United Nations Framework Convention on Climate Change." 1998. <http://unfccc.int/resource/docs/convkp/kpeng.pdf>.

Other O Books — www.obooks.com
5744 Presley Way, Oakland, CA 94618
Distributed by SPD: 1341 Seventh Street, Berkeley, CA 94710

Towards The Primeval Lightning Field, Will Alexander, $12.00
Horace, Tim Atkins, $12.00
Return of the World, Todd Baron, $10.00
A Certain Slant of Sunlight, Ted Berrigan, $12.00
Mob, Abigail Child, $12.00
CYMK, Michael Coffey, $14.00
Debts and Obligations, Alicia Cohen, $12.00
Moira, Norma Cole, $12.00
It Then, Danielle Collobert, $10.00
Parcel, Sarah Ann Cox, $12.00
Lapses, John Crouse, $10.00
Headlines, John Crouse, $12.00
The Arcades, Michael Davidson, $12.00
Candor, Alan Davies, $10.00
iduna, kari edwards, $12.00
Rome, A Mobile Home, Jerry Estrin,
    Roof Books and Potes & Poets with O Books, $9.00
Turn Left in Order to Go Right, Norman Fischer, $12.00
Time Rations, Benjamin Friedlander, $12.00
Startle Response, Heather Fuller, $12.00
byt, William Fuller, $12.00
The Sugar Borders, William Fuller, $12.00
DeathStar/Ricochet, Judith Goldman, $14.00
War and Peace 2, eds. Judith Goldman and Leslie Scalapino, $14.00
War and Peace 3, eds. Judith Goldman and Leslie Scalapino, $14.00
Phantom Anthems, Robert Grenier, $12.00
What I Believe Transpiration/Transpiring Minnesota, Robert Grenier, $24.00
The Inveterate Life, Jessica Grim, $12.00
Fray, Jessica Grim, $12.00
Music or Forgetting, E. Tracy Grinnell, $12.00
Some Clear Souvenir, E. Tracy Grinnell, $12.00
Memory Play, Carla Harryman, $9.00
The Words/ after Carl Sandburg's Rootabaga Stories and Jean-Paul Sartre,
    Carla Harryman, $12.00
The Quietist, Fanny Howe, $9.00
Around Sea, Brenda Iijima, $12.00
VEL, P. Inman, $12.00

60 lv Bo(e)mbs, Paolo Javier, $12.00
The History of the Loma People, Paul D. Korvah, $12.00
248 mgs., a panic picnic, Susan Landers, $12.00
Curve, Andrew Levy, $12.00
Values Chauffeur You, Andrew Levy, $12.00
Dreaming Close By, Rick London, $12.00
Abjections, Rick London, $5.00
Dissuasion Crowds the Slow Worker, Lori Lubeski, $10.00
Plum Stones/Cartoons of No Heaven, Michael McClure, $13.00
The Case, Laura Moriarty, $12.00
Home on the Range (The Night Sky with Stars in My Mouth),
    Tenney Nathanson, $12.00
Criteria, Sianne Ngai, $11.00
Close to me & Closer ... (The Language of Heaven) and Désamère,
    Alice Notley, $12.00
Catenary Odes, Ted Pearson, $12.00
Collision Center, Randall Potts, $12.00
Light, Jerry Ratch, $12.00
(where late the sweet) BIRDS SANG, Stephen Ratcliffe, $12.00
Tottering State, Tom Raworth, $15.00
Kismet, Pat Reed, $12.00
Cold Heaven, Camille Roy, $12.00
The Seven Voices, Lisa Samuels, $12.00
Crowd and not evening or light, Leslie Scalapino, $12.00
Enough, an anthology, ed. Leslie Scalapino and Rick London, $16.00
O ONE/AN ANTHOLOGY, ed. Leslie Scalapino, $12.00
O TWO/AN ANTHOLOGY: What is the inside, what is outside?,
    ed. Leslie Scalapino, $12.00
O/4: Subliminal Time, ed. Leslie Scalapino, $12.00
War and Peace, ed. Leslie Scalapino, $14.00
The India Book: Essays and Translations, Andrew Schelling, $12.00
"...But I Couldn't Speak...", Jono Schneider, $12.00
Rumors of Buildings To Live In, Keith Shein, $12.00
A's Dream, Aaron Shurin, $12.00
Partisans, Rodrigo Toscano, $12.00
Lilyfoil, Elizabeth Treadwell, $12.00
trespasses, Padcha Tuntha-Obas, $12.00
Homing Devices, Liz Waldner, $12.00
Picture of The Picture of The Image in The Glass, Craig Watson, $12.00